# Contents

Preface

Introduction

**PART I: Vehicles of Knowledge**     1

Reason     3

Perception     11

Intuition     17

Language and Meaning     23

**PART II: Worlds of Knowledge**     31

Mathematics     33

Natural Sciences     41

Human Sciences     51

History     61

Languages and Literature     67

Ethics     75

Aesthetics     85

Acknowledgements     91

# Preface

This book is for students following the Theory of Knowledge (ToK) course in the International Baccalaureate. Its aims are to introduce pupils to the subject and to outline ways of approaching the world of knowledge.

I should make it clear that this is not a text book. One of the great strengths of the course is that it makes such a mundane thing impossible. This is because every student is unique and every student will carry out their own exploration of the world of knowledge in their own way. A text book would need to be infinitely long to be of any use - and being infinitely long would make it useless.

The world of knowledge can seem very strange and forbidding to the outsider: a world populated by ideas that, though fascinating, may also be challenging and disturbing. Entering this world, and getting the most out of the experience, demands an open mind and a willingness to accept, at least initially, that other minds may see things differently.

Hence, this book is more like a guide book. Dipping into it before setting off may prepare you for unpleasant surprises or whet your appetite for the novelties ahead. It might also provide a useful reference point if you feel a little bit lost at some stage in your journey. But it is just a primer. All it will give you is rudimentary information about the world of knowledge and point out some of the sights worth seeing. More important to your ToK course will be your fellow-students and your teachers, acting as visitors and guides themselves. Most important of all will be you: an interested traveller can make all exotic.

# Introduction

This book has two parts. The first part consists of four 'vehicles of knowledge'. These are the fundamental ways that we use to acquire and build up our knowledge as well as being the means of getting to new worlds. It may be that each 'vehicle' is suited to the different types of 'terrain' that you will find in the worlds of knowledge that you are exploring. Knowing something about their strength, scope and limitations is needed before tackling more specific areas; so read these before going into part two. This second part contains seven sections on individual subject areas within the IB programme. These can be read in any order at all. Divisions between these subject areas is fairly arbitrary; they are part of a continuum of knowledge without natural boundaries. The order in which I have put them is a personal whim. I see them as going from greater certainty to greater doubt on the one hand, and from simplicity to complexity on the other. I'm sure that many will disagree.

As far as possible, I have refrained from mentioning any belief that involves the supernatural. This is not because such beliefs are unimportant - after all, they inform and constrain the lives of the majority of people in the world. The reason is that, to me, faith and critical thinking are not comfortably reconciled. If you have no faith, you will not wonder at its omission. If you *do* have faith you can consider any 'truth' achieved by critical thinking in the book to be a subset of a 'divine' truth. In other words, the absence of supernatural belief should make no difference to anyone.

If you think you have found an original idea in this book, then either you or I have made a mistake. I have simply brought together some of the thoughts of those who have questioned what knowledge is all about. I have avoided naming these people for two reasons. Firstly, I wanted to emphasise the ideas alone without importing other baggage like 'He's a great thinker so is likely to be right' or 'He's ancient so is likely to be wrong'. The merits of *the ideas themselves* are all you should consider and not putting a name to them should help with this. (Given this spirit of a genuine wish to promote thinking, I am confident the thinkers concerned will not mind being unacknowledged.) Secondly, it makes things too easy for the lazy student who will simply lift an idea with the name of a Great Thinker attached to it and plonk it into their argument without much thought. This is a guide to the world of thought, not a handbook of ideas to cut and paste.

For exactly the same reasons I have put no quotes in the book (apart from the one from a genius who is not regarded as a philosopher in the classical sense). But I *have* put a proverb at the start of each section. This is a challenge. Proverbs are referred to as 'folk wisdom' (or as 'peasant philosophy' depending on your generosity of spirit). After reading each section you should be able to see why each proverb contains some merit but little truth.

Lastly, you are bound to detect bias in the way I have presented ideas. I am comfortable with this. Although I have made attempts to disguise my own beliefs among the ideas in this book, and give a fair chance to ones I feel are wrong or silly, I think you may well find it easier to argue with a more personal presentation than with a more standard, 'text-book' one. One of my beliefs is that argument (or discussion) helps define and develop good sense. Thus, I hope you find this book provoking.

# PART I
*Vehicles of Knowledge*

# REASON

*There is reason in the roasting of eggs.*


Physically, there is very little that is special about humans. Mentally, most of what happens isn't all that special either. There is one thing, however, that humans do that no other species does, not even the really clever ones like chimps and dolphins: we ask 'why?'

Animals can be trained to show how intelligent they are. Examples would include carrying out a sequence of complicated tasks, or manipulating language-symbols to answer questions and to make statements. A chimp can be asked to retrieve a banana from some inaccessible place. It might try to get it; it may not bother. It doesn't think 'why?' Ask a young child to do something and you may well be asked 'why?' The child wants a reason.

**Answering a why question**
Pick any statement you like. Ask the question 'why?' Answer the question. Ask 'why?' again. Keep repeating the process for as long as you can. You'll probably find you can't get much further than about four successive answers. Let's try it:

*"The weather's nice today."*
*"Why?"*
*"Because it is sunny."*
*"Why?"*
*"Because there is no cloud cover."*
*"Why?"*
*"Because the relative temperature, pressure and saturation of the air above us means that water molecules have not aggregated into droplets."*
*"Why?"*

*"It's a natural law."*
*"Why?"*
*"Your guess is as good as mine - or anyone else's."*

And there is nowhere else to go - we've run out of reasons for the nice weather and, if we were to continue, would be looking for reasons for relative strengths of guesswork and so on.

Reasons are explanations. They give an account of something which fits in with our view of the world. That is not to say that reasons are always correct because that depends on how good our view of the world is. If we believe in a world in which fairies, gnomes, wicked witches and magic castles are entirely credible, then:

*"Why did Cinderella meet the charming Prince?"*
Could be satisfactorily answered with:
*"Her fairy godmother enchanted various animals and vegetables."*

However, the more we reason about things, the less satisfied we become with reasons like the last one. We want our reasons to be *true*.

**Reasoning and truth**
Reasoning is the process we go through to produce satisfactory explanations. What gives us confidence that our reasoning about something is *true*? Here we hit a tough philosophical problem: What is truth? The simple answer to this is: *"The truth is what is the real, the actual, state of things. We can check our reasons by checking with the physical world out there. If you say 'The weather's nice' and I look out of the window and see that it is sunny, then what you say is true."* This definition of truth depends on there being a physical world of facts that exists independently of our mental world. If this assumption is true, then all we have to do to get at the truth is to compare our mental world with the physical world and see if they agree. If they do, then our reasoning is spot on; if they don't, then we need

to try again perhaps after collecting a few more facts.

To me, this seems such a beautiful bit of reasoning that it's a pity that someone had to ask *'Why?'* But someone did and it's hard to give them a good reason in reply. The difficulty is that 'the real, the actual, state of things' which we think of as existing independent of our minds can only be thought of when we have taken it into our minds in the first place. Thus, the world we think of *has* to be a *mental* world - the only way we could get out and think about the 'real, physical' world would be not to think at all!

Is there a good answer to this problem? It seems that most philosophers agree that the best answer is as follows: Our mental world is shaped by the belief that the thoughts we have *represent* some real, physical world. In other words we have *objective* thoughts and these apply to the real, physical world. If we try to make these objective thoughts nice and orderly then we generate an objective world which is the nearest we are ever going to get to the real thing.

Having revealed that in this part of knowledge there is a lot of deep and scary water, I leave it to you and other hardy explorers to pull on the scuba gear if you like. I'm heading back to firmer ground.

**Pure reason**
This is a way of acquiring knowledge that will strike you as blindingly obvious. The main attraction of it is that you don't have to make any reference to what I've been calling the physical world at all. Indeed, without this sort of knowledge you cannot begin to make sense of any objective (and physical) world at all. By this I mean that before you can make sense of any information that comes into your mind there has to be a set of basic beliefs about how things are. If you don't have this set of basic beliefs, then it would be impossible to begin thinking in the first place. Such beliefs include the fundamentals of arithmetic (which I'll turn to in more detail in the 'Mathematics' section); logical statements and principles; the belief

that an event has to have a cause; the belief that there are laws of nature that can be discovered; the belief that people and other objects occupy a particular place and that they persist in time. As I say, all these things seem so obvious that there seems little point in questioning them.

Asking ourselves if these basic beliefs are *true* or not threatens to take us back to the deep waters of the previous section. Perhaps we can be satisfied with just accepting that this is how the *mind* is and, as before, acknowledging that, although we can be certain of some of the things in our mind, we cannot ever be equally certain about what we'd call the physical world. Such basic beliefs are as true for us as anything can be. But the question we might ask is: Is *my* set of basic beliefs the same as *yours*? Do we all reason in the same way?

The answer must be '*yes*'; reasoning is universal (we all do it the same way) and objective (and, if we are careful, will get the same answer). However, the reason why it must be 'yes' isn't so straightforward as we might like. That's because it isn't an explanation of why it is so, it's an explanation of why it cannot be any other way.

Some people say that reason is always going to be subjective because we have only our own thoughts about which we can be sure; you cannot be equally sure about the processes of thought going on inside anyone else's head. Thus, the 'truth' that I have about things is just my truth. Your 'truth' may be different and as valid as any other person's 'truth'. This must be wrong because it doesn't make sense. Consider this:

**Andrew:** *"Everybody has their own version of the truth."*
**Barbara:** *"I think that people share the same truth."*

If what Andrew has said is true, then what Barbara has said must be true (since she is one of the 'everybody'). But if what Barbara says is true then Andrew must be wrong. On the other hand, if what Barbara has said is true then what Andrew has said must be false, i.e.

Andrew must be wrong.

In short, Andrew's argument proves itself wrong. Notice that this doesn't prove that Barbara is right (that there is objective truth). But it *does* show that the counter-argument is not right.

A more compelling argument for reason being universal is that no matter what arguments are ranged against it, these arguments themselves must appeal to reason. Someone might say *"We reason as we do because that is the way our culture has brought us up"*. However, we can still ask such a person *"**Why** do we?"* And ultimately the answer they give us will be using reason and not using a cultural explanation. Even if they answer *"Because that's how our culture has brought us up"* can you see that this is a *reasonable* explanation rather than a cultural one?

Reason is the absolute end of the line. We cannot question reason except by using reason. And if you refuse to use reason, you are mad.

**Reasoning and Logic**
Logic is all about reasons and reasoning. It is concerned with reasons for believing and its central task is to establish whether something is valid or not. Being valid is not the same as being true but, as you will see, perhaps it gets us as close as we could possibly be to the truth.

What separates logic from other sorts of reasoning is most easily demonstrated by using a couple of examples. Imagine a virgin male aged 20. Why is he celibate? We might reply that he is celibate because he was brought up in a strict household where obedience to the moral code of the Bible was instilled in him and that these lessons were reinforced by his school and church. This is a reasonable explanation for his celibacy but it is not strictly logical. Contrast the above with this:

A man believes the following:
1. *Having sexual relations outside marriage is wrong.*
2. *I am unmarried.*
3. *I do no wrong.*
Therefore, *I am celibate.*

Just by looking at the man's beliefs we can see that his celibacy *must* follow from them. (Notice that we do not have to share his beliefs - and they may not all be true. But neither of these considerations affects the logic.) We would say that the man has a *good reason* for being celibate. This would not be the case for the following, however:

A man believes the following:
1. *Most unmarried people are celibate.*
2. *That woman is unmarried.*
Therefore, *she is celibate.*

Here the conclusion is a *bad reason* because it does not necessarily follow. (In logic, necessarily means 'must certainly always and forever be'.) She may be celibate, but further evidence is needed because the evidence of these beliefs alone are not enough to guarantee it.

A simple test for whether a conclusion is valid or invalid (i.e. a good reason or a bad reason) is to ask *"Can the beliefs be true and yet the conclusion be false?"* We can answer '*yes*' to the second example and this shows it is invalid. In general, an argument is valid if it is impossible for all the beliefs set out initially to be true and yet the conclusion be false. Thus, if:

1. *All books without pictures are dull.*
2. *This is a book without pictures.*
Therefore, *this is a dull book.*

The conclusion is perfectly valid (and may even be true).

Logic is built up from principles that are self-evidently true. It would be impossible to imagine that anyone could disagree with the logic in the previous example (provided they understood the meaning of the sentences, of course). Or that the logical identity of *'A dog is a dog'* is open to question. Or that we can have two statements like *'He is male'* and *'He is not male'* being both true for one and the same person at one and the same time. The inconsistency of the last logical principle is often made use of when we try to change someone's belief. We might argue: *'Look, you think all teachers are boring, don't you? And you agree Mr Brown's a teacher, right? And yet you say he's interesting! Make up your mind!'* We would expect that merely by pointing out these statements that it is obvious that Mr Brown cannot be interesting. Further argument would be unnecessary.

The purpose of logic is to take statements (or 'propositions') and determine their consistency using such logical rules and principles as those above. To achieve this, logic uses symbolic notation to stand for beliefs and the ways of manipulating them. This is mathematical because quantity is involved - from 'a' through 'some' and 'most' to 'all'.

There was great hope early in the 20th century that logical analysis could be brought to bear upon all our statements of belief; just fit the belief into the appropriate equation, press the button and, hey presto, out pops the answer 'valid' or 'not valid'. Unfortunately, natural language has not proved as tractable as had been hoped. Thus logic uses artificial language which gets as close to our natural language as it can. In doing this it has made great contributions towards clarifying and demystifying certain ways of thinking. It is a powerful tool for laying bare weaknesses in argument, false beliefs and inconsistent thinking. It is, perhaps, not sophisticated enough to make us confident that we are nearer the truth by using it (as yet?), but it is invaluable for cutting away past daftness.

## Practical reason

In this sort of reasoning we relax the requirement for certainty. We have to do this because we want to extend our knowledge beyond the certainties that we can derive from areas such as mathematics and logic. Our world consists of other areas which are of great importance to us such as science, arts and ethics. We want answers to the question 'why?' in these areas too and reasoning has proved to be a powerful way of getting them.

What limits reason to something less than certainty outside maths and logic has to do with the quality of the input and the range of possible outcomes that could result. '*2 + 2*', for example, is a top-quality input because we can be certain of each of the things in it (each '*2*' and the '*+*' could not be mistaken or confused). Likewise '*= 4*' is the only possible outcome (it cannot be wrong). But '*humans and chimps share a common ancestor*' has far more in its contents that can be questioned; and so '*because they both have many genes in common*' is less certain: there may be other explanations for the similarities. And further still '*Bach and Beethoven are great composers*' is far less obviously followed by '*because their music has such scope for re-interpretation*'; and '*Killing people is wrong*' is not always justified by '*because human life is sacrosanct*'.

That said, even if certainty eludes us, we do look for satisfactory explanations - reasons - for such things. This is what we call practical reason; explanations that help us live our lives more fully. We want to understand the world. We want to have confidence that our explanations of the world approach (even if they don't coincide with) the truth. Reasoning has proved the best way for making consistent sense of the world.

Finally, the great thing about reason is that can be used to challenge any authority. You can keep asking '*Why?*' until the authority gives you a satisfactory explanation, tells you that you are too stupid to understand, or shuts you up. You assert your humanity when you demand to know '*Why?*'

# PERCEPTION

*All is fish that comes to the net.*

That we can gain knowledge through our senses seems so obvious that, at first, it may be hard to see that there are any difficulties here at all. One way to help you see that there *are* difficulties is to get you to abandon this world and travel to another...

Imagine that you wake up on a space-ship. You have been in suspended animation and have travelled to a distant galaxy. The space-ship crashes onto a planet. Looking out of the observation ports you see nothing but total blackness. You use the space-ship's instrumentation to assess the external environment. Bizarrely, outside the space-ship there is a blank in the part of the electro-magnetic spectrum that causes the light-sensitive cells in your eye to respond. There are plenty of other waves out there but you can't see them. How strange. But it gets stranger. There is also a blank in the spectrum of sound waves that exactly corresponds with the sound-waves your ears are sensitive to. There are plenty of other waves out there but you can't hear them. As your instruments scan through other physical properties you discover that this planet, besides being invisible and inaudible to you, cannot be tasted, smelt or felt. Nonetheless, the planet exists out there. It's just that *your* senses can't detect it.

You turn to your super-computer and programme it to convert the electro-magnetic and sound waves that are coming from the features of the planet into ones which your senses *can* appreciate. You instruct the computer to produce a complete hologram of the surface of the world and to project it in the Viewing Room.

You travel for several minutes down miles of corridors and enter a vast, silent, empty, windowless space: the Viewing Room. You stand in the middle of the Room and utter the traditional command "*Let there be light*!" The computer instantly projects the hologram and the Viewing Room is filled with the image of the surface of the planet. You gaze around slowly. There are weird, fascinating shapes and colours and sounds and smells surrounding you. This is a fantastic, an amazing, a wonderful world.

But is the hologram a *true* representation of the planet you are on? The images that you are getting in the Viewing Room are *interpretations* of signals from the outside. You cannot possibly check that the computer has got it all right, that the shapes, colours, sounds and so on are a true match with the signals that its sensors are picking up from the actual planet's surface. That's because you, as a human, do not have the necessary *extra*-sensory perception required to carry out such a check (how could you see if the colour blue was really there if you can't detect the colour blue?). The hologram may appear extremely '*life-like*' but, in the end, it is only an image.

Now, let's return to Earth.

Look around you. What do you see? Obviously, you see a small part of the planet Earth. Where, precisely, do you 'see' this small part of the planet Earth? You will probably answer 'inside my brain'. This is because you know that light from the part of the planet around you enters your eyes and is converted into electrical impulses. These then pass into the brain where a picture of the world is projected into your brain's equivalent of the Viewing Room. But where exactly is this Viewing Room? The answer is astonishing: it's *outside* your brain. Your brain projects its 'hologram' of the planet Earth as if your eyes were two projectors and the space *outside* your brain and body were a room. To us it appears that we are peering out at the world through the observation ports we call eyes. But, of course, eyeballs are opaque when seen from behind. Our brain creates an illusion that we are looking at the real world. In fact, we are experiencing the brain's interpretations of the outside world which it projects outwards to give us the impression that a real world exists 'out there'. In a real sense, we make up the world as we go along.

Before reading on, give yourself a few minutes to reflect on this remarkable aspect of your brain-power. Fully appreciating that what you have been thinking of as the world 'out there' is really an image that your brain is creating for you will almost certainly be startling, unsettling, thrilling and amazing.

\* \* \* \*

Right. Now let's get down to earth. What implications does all this have for our gaining of knowledge? Perhaps the most fundamental question we could ask would be "*How can I know that there is a real world out there at all?*" As in the story about the distant planet and the Viewing Room, we cannot check our senses are working properly because we need our senses to do the checking. Clearly, this is impossible - like trying to check the accuracy of a thermometer using only the thermometer itself.

One answer to this problem would be: We all confirm that a real world exists out there, independent of our brains, because we always agree in our 'projections'. When I am looking at a chair, everyone else around will agree that they too see the chair. This may prompt a deeper thought: "*How do I know other people are real? Couldn't they also be just images my brain is making up?*" This is a possibility but hardly a real one. If it were true, then you would have, for example, created all the world's great music and paintings, written all of Shakespeare's works, discovered penicillin, invented the computer, etc., etc. This is hard to claim, even for the vainest of us. (However, if you meet someone who *does* claim all this, then do feel free to insult them in the most withering terms: they will have to believe that they are insulting themselves since you are just a figment of their imagination.)

## The brain

Another approach to the problem would be to look at the brain itself to discover how it works and generates its images. If we find that it has a simple mechanism, where cause and effect are related in a straight-forward way, then this would give us some confidence that it is an honest interpreter of reality. Leaving aside the difficulty of checking a brain with a brain (the 'thermometer problem' again), when we look into a skull we find a mass of tiny, soft, wet, grey cells - no pictures of worlds or anything like it. In my analogy with the space-ship it would be like opening up the super-computer: there would be no pictures inside it either. To try to find out how the brain does its stuff you have to fiddle with it as you might do if you were told to find out how the supercomputer works; bash keys, stick a screw-driver into its innards, monitor the flow of electricity between components, slosh in varying amounts of power, experiment with the input and output ports and see if you can deduce any links between what you do and what happens on the screen. By doing these sorts of things, neuroscientists have helped towards an explanation of how the brain works. They have also discovered that the perception our brains have of the world can be mistaken.

## False perception

The first problem lies with our sensory equipment. It is not perfect. Sometimes it will send a message to the brain when it has not received an appropriate signal; sometimes it will send a message but the brain never receives it. An example of the first is a persistent ringing sound in the ears for several hours after prolonged exposure to loud sounds. An example of the second is the chemical blocking of the nerve pathway by some anaesthetic or other. So, our senses are not entirely trustworthy but these examples will probably illustrate that it takes something fairly exceptional to make the input signals to the brain false ones.

A second problem lies in the mysterious something that we call 'consciousness' though we aren't certain what it is, let alone how it works. It's not necessary for us to tackle this brute direct, but we will have to cast a swift glance in its direction because of its relationship to knowledge. This is particularly true of the sort of knowledge that we like to think we can *decide* to think about: conscious knowledge. Of all the millions of bits of information that flow into our brains every second only a small proportion enters our conscious mind so that we become aware of it. The rest (or nearly all of it anyway) gets lost. The 'decision' as to which bits of information enter our conscious mind is sometimes (or often) taken *sub*consciously. Thus, the subconscious mind monitors the incoming signals and 'decides' which ones are important enough to send to the conscious mind. A simple illustration of this is the crowded room where many people are, like you, chatting to friends. While you listen to your friend, everyone else's conversation makes a background buzz. Suddenly, you hear your name mentioned nearby and look round to see who is talking about you. For this sort of thing to happen your brain must have been monitoring *all* the conversations within earshot. For most of the time nothing of interest was coming in and so the subconscious brain toned it down to a buzz. Then, something important to you cropped up - *your name was mentioned* - and your subconscious immediately made you aware of it. Hence, the knowledge that you get into your conscious brain (the knowledge you *perceive*) passes through a subconscious process that we seem to have little, if any, control over. This is a bit limiting: we may be losing potential knowledge all the time because our subconscious is rejecting it as unimportant or 'boring'. (This might be why schoolwork is so hard.)

Two further problems in perception are ambiguity and illusion. Sometimes the brain receives information that is capable of being interpreted in more than one way: it is ambiguous. We are usually aware that there are more ways of interpreting the information and can resolve the problem by looking for more data. But are we always aware that a certain piece of perceived information *is* ambiguous? Might we just accept what we perceive as being the case? A simple example is the Moon which looks like a disc and like a sphere - it could be either as we view it from Earth. Most of us are confident that it is a sphere but it is not hard to imagine that a few thousand years ago this possibility had not even been thought of. Just as the possibility that the moon is the end of a long tube that points at us like the barrel of a gun may not have crossed your mind until now; but it is another interpretation. This is another way of saying that our knowledge is incomplete.

An illusion is the result of the brain receiving perfectly adequate information but which it then 'distorts' to fit in with its expectations: it expects the world out there to conform to certain patterns, and incoming information is moulded to fit. There are many visual illusions which confirm that this is so. Our concern here is that we may be counting some things as 'knowledge' when they are illusions. One tentative answer to this concern is to say that if our knowledge of the world were illusory in any important degree then we would have made lots of mistakes in the past and not survived in the Darwinian struggle for existence. The fact that we are here is a strong affirmation that the world is as we perceive it.

# INTUITION

*It is idle to swallow a cow and choke on its tail.*


Apart from reason and perception, what I am calling intuition is another way of gaining knowledge of the world. It has been described as emotional, or irrational, or nonrational, thinking but, since these terms carry rather negative overtones, I prefer the term intuition. I would define it as *unguided* thinking. This distinguishes it from reason (which is objective and open to rational argument) and from perception (which deals with the relationship between our minds and the rest of the world). I would say that it is unguided because it seems that we cannot *generate* such thinking nor exercise much, if any, control over where it leads us.

Some examples of intuitive thinking would include: feeling what sort of behaviour is right; appreciating the beauty of an object; betting on a certain number because you know it is going to come up. It is often regarded as the sort of thinking that separates human beings from other forms of life and, indeed, from machines which might be capable of perceiving the world and reasoning about it in the same way as we do. Many see it as integral to such things as creativity, imagination, wonder, love and euphoria; with guilt, anguish, fear, hate and horror. But most of all, it is generally associated with free will, the sense we have that we can determine what we are going to do in the world. Thus, it is of great significance to us all.

Intuitive thinking has a distinguished pedigree. Homer's heroes were inspired and informed by it. It has often been associatied with the most exalted areas of human achievement including poetry, art, music - indeed, 'humanity' itself. In the modern world it still exercises a powerful influence over our every-day lives when we are 'being ourselves' or 'listening to our inner voice'. Though intuition has usually been linked with what is called 'spirit', it does not necessarily have a supernatural dimension and so may be legitimately considered in the ToK course where critical thinking is central.

**Where is the intuitive world?**
Rational thinking - reason - is associated with the head (and specifically the brain). Intuitive thinking (especially in the past) has been associated with other parts of the body. Someone can 'know in their heart' or 'feel it in their bones' or have a 'gut reaction' or say their 'blood was up'. These forms of speech indicate that we respond to certain things without the thinking we associate with the 'cold, clear' reasoning of the brain. These are often *emotional* responses either to the world outside or to our own private thoughts. But although nowadays it is acknowledged that emotional responses are situated in the brain and not anywhere else in the body, they still seem separable from reason, still seem to occupy a different sort of world from reason.

**Where do our intuitions come from?**
One possibility is that our intuitions are with us from birth. Here the idea of a supernatural spirit might account for them. But since this cannot be sensibly questioned I will leave it to one side. Alternatively, the idea of genetic programming might do the same. It appears that many people have been persuaded that humans are merely 'lumbering robots' at the mercy of a blueprint in DNA that determines all aspects of their bodies and behaviour. Evidence in favour of this might be that all humans have this type of thinking: it seems to be a part of our fundamental nature. And other social animals (which also have DNA) also have emotional thinking. They can suffer delight and distress in the same way. Finally, we know that genes exert a powerful influence on the way our bodies (including our brains) are made and why should the attribute 'behaviour' not be similarly determined since it is central to our survival in the real world?

A second possibility is that we 'learn' our intuitions. I've put the learn in inverted commas because this is not in the formal sense of learning. Not many people would argue that intuitive thinking can be taught in the same way that, say, geography is taught to us. We may be born with no intuitions at all, but when we are growing up we could learn them from picking up what is the dominant response to a situation from those around us. If they seem delighted at the prospect of a good meal, we imitate this delight and come to learn that this is the appropriate response. If our group is distressed by some event, we copy the mannerisms and expressions of our elders and come to share in that communal feeling and, later, transfer this feeling to ourselves as individuals. Thus, intuitive thinking is a sort of social or cultural conditioning that short-circuits reasoning. Evidence in favour of this might be that different human cultures at different periods in history have different styles and emphases within their intuitive thinking. This implies that intuitive thinking is far more flexible than genes and genetic selection would allow; that this knowledge is a part of the knowledge of the group rather than of the individual. Hence it is not exposed to natural selection at the level of the gene as advocated by those who promote the supremacy of DNA.

A third possibility is that intuitive thinking is an accidental remnant of our evolutionary past. During our species' evolution our brains got much larger (at the rate of about two tablespoonfuls per 100 000 years, i.e. the rate of increase was not especially startling). It is assumed that they got larger because something about a larger brain is an advantage. But it might have been that only *part* of the brain was the truly advantageous bit. And the simplest way to make this part bigger would be to just increase the size of the whole thing. Rather like, say, if it were advantageous to have a thumb twice as long as it is, the easiest solution for development is to make *the whole hand* twice as big. This means your fingers have got unnecessarily bigger but, so what, look at this wonderful thumb! In this theory you might envisage the part of the brain that is used for, say, memory as being the one where it would be a real advantage to increase it in size. But puffing up the whole brain also means that other areas, like those to do with intuitive thinking, get larger too - larger than necessary, in fact. At this point they dominate the individual's thinking but, so long as there is no other type of thinking that works so well, it doesn't matter. The other type of thinking, the type we have but which seems to be undeveloped or absent in other species, would be reasoning - and this is probably a relatively recent innovation.

These two types of thinking, reasoning and intuition, will often be in conflict. Reasoning is slow, hard but relatively sure. Intuition is quick, easy but open to much doubt. Perhaps our struggle towards knowledge consists of the battle between our 'natural' thinking (intuition) which insists on the quickest, easiest response to a problem, and reasoning which demands reflection, rigour and evidence. Perhaps the 'unnecessarily well-developed' intuitive parts of the brain need to be subdued by reason for us to make progress in our knowledge. Far from being 'what make us human' intuitions may be regarded as 'what keep us brutish'.

**Implications of intuitive thinking**
If our intuitions are inborn then we cannot escape them. If they are 'natural' in this sense then it could be argued that we should pay far more attention to them because we will then be 'in tune' with how our minds are naturally. Then we will be more comfortable with ourselves and each other. Allowing our innate sense of intuitive thinking free reign will tap into our creativity to a much greater extent and hence improve those attributes of humanity that distinguish us so remarkably - our music, language, art and 'soul'. Reasoning should then be given a secondary role, kept for mundane tasks like working out the optimal plumbing configuration for a house, or the sequence of putting the parts together. The house as a whole should be purely inspirational. This flies in the face of modern Western thinking about development and progress; but who is to say we have gone about things the right way? Just look at the sorts of houses we live in!

Alternatively, if we *learn* our intuitions from those around us as we grow up, then it is clearly of great importance that those most closely concerned with our upbringing recognise this. We need to learn the appropriate sorts of intuitions (like being kind to weaker members of society) rather than inappropriate ones (like viewing foreigners with suspicion). This puts a much greater burden on parents, teachers and other adults to ensure the 'intuitive environment' is kept optimal for this social engineering of children's intuition.

If intuitive thinking is overblown with respect to reason then we ought to suppress it wherever possible and seek the rational explanation always. Reason should be regarded as paramount, intuition as fundamentally flawed. Our social institutions should then be geared towards this end and any tendencies to veer away from reasoning should be discouraged, if not outlawed. Again, this is heretical with respect to current social norms; but hasn't reason proved itself to be the *best* approach to solving problems in the past?

# LANGUAGE AND MEANING

*Every cock will crow upon his own dunghill.*

So far, I have looked at knowledge that has been gained through reason, knowledge gained through our senses in perception, and knowledge that seems to be grasped intuitively 'in our hearts'. This leaves a whole lot of knowledge that enters our brain in the form of words - by people telling us things, or by our reading about things. These words are part of a language which we ourselves use (with more or less fluency) to contribute to the spread of knowledge. Since it is so crucial to our knowledge of the world, it is necessary to ask: What is language and how does it work?

**The Meaning of Language**
The first thing to point out is that human language - using words - is quite different from the sort of communication used by other species in the wild. Initially, you might think that the hoots, clicks, roars and chattering of chimpanzees constitute a language along the same lines of the sort we use, but this is not the case. For one thing, the chimpanzees do not use their language creatively; a hoot means just one thing, it cannot be 'expressed' in another sort of hoot. The sounds they make are not constantly re-ordered, re-combined and re-interpreted; they are often just repeated: a hoot's a hoot's a hoot. For another thing, humans can be seen as having *two* sorts of communication: one like other species and, in addition, language proper. The first sort would include what is called body language (posture and gesture) and facial expressions for things like joy and sadness as well as sounds like laughter and sobbing. These forms of communication are quite different from language: they are 'natural'; they are emotional responses over which we have little control; they are shared by all humans (and some of them by other species too - we can see when a chimp is sad). When we ask about such emotions we often hear: "*I*

*can't put my feelings into words"*. This phrase reveals that the two forms of communication are parallel and different and only translatable to a limited extent.

Human language is thus a special way of communicating between individuals. It uses words. [I shall leave other forms of symbolic representation to the section on Languages and Literature.] These words are symbols that have a certain meaning, and this meaning is taken as referring to something in the world we share with other humans. Words are usually grouped together to make statements. The statements convey something from one person to another and these statements are generally aimed at the true state of affairs in the world.

**What do words mean?**
This looks a simple question to answer: look up the definition in a dictionary. Thus, *circle* means 'a plane figure bounded by one line every point of which is equally distant from a fixed point called the centre'. But what do the words in the definition mean? Again, we could look them all up ( 'a', 'plane', 'figure', 'bounded', and so on) and produce an even longer sentence. But this too would be made up of words and we could repeat the question and get an even longer sentence made up of words... From this you can see that defining words by words can only be circular: at some point a word must have a *direct* meaning - as if I were leaning over your shoulder pointing at the letter o and saying "***This*** *is a circle"*.

Getting a direct meaning out of a word is not so easy. We don't have people pointing out objects in the world and naming them for us all the time. (And who told *them* the word in the first place?) Let's take the word *dog* as an example. We've all seen dogs and we all know what the word means. If I said: "*I was teaching one day when a dog ran into the room*", although you wouldn't know the precise colour, size, shape and so on of the particular dog that had enlivened the lesson, you would know what sort of animal it must have been. You can easily talk about dogs quite meaningfully without knowing the precise definition of the word *dog*. (This neatly demonstrates that meaning and definition are different.) So where did your meaning of the word dog come from and why is it exactly the same meaning as mine?

You will have learned the word *dog* by being shown certain examples, but these examples will have been different from the ones I was shown, so we cannot be thinking of the same examples when we use the word. Also, we can use the word to mean *all dogs* - including those in the future - when we say something like: "*One day there will be more dogs on Mars than on Earth.*" This suggests that the link between the word *dog* and all the dogs that have existed, do exist, and will exist in the Universe, is *indirect*, that there is something that links the word *dog* with *all dogs*. But what sort of thing could this be?

Is it the *idea* of a dog? If the answer is '*yes*', we can ask two further questions: Is this idea in your mind? Or is the idea outside your mind but consisting of something that your mind somehow can latch onto? If it were in your mind, then it seems unlikely, to say the least, that all the rest of us have produced the self-same idea such that we each know what the other is talking about. The second possibility would seem more likely since we can all latch onto the idea in the same way and so be able to talk meaningfully about dogs. But this is no real solution to the problem of *dog* meaning *all dogs*. All we have now is the *idea of dog* meaning *all dogs* and we're no nearer saying how the *idea of dog* links one with all.

The meaning of a word is thus something of a mystery because it doesn't seem to be able to be pinned down to anything; not to the examples, not to the word itself, not to the individual mind, not to a separate idea floating between the word and all the things to which it refers. That said, we can just accept that this is a problem (and perhaps even dismiss it as trivial - isn't it blindingly obvious that a dog is a dog after all?) and go on to something meatier.

Once we understand the word *dog* we have acquired some real knowledge - we understand that it refers to one, or a type of, object in the world that has four legs, pointed ears and barks. We can use it to communicate ideas to others like 'My dog is very loyal' or 'Dogs smell bad when they get wet'. If you grasp this idea then you will appreciate that the meaning of a word is governed by *how it is used by everyone* - if words meant different things to different people then coherent communication would be impossible.

Of course, sometimes we want to alter or modify an existing word - usually to be more precise. Thus the physicist uses the word 'force' in a particular and very precise way when she wishes to say what it would take to accelerate a mass by a given amount. She might force you to write down the equation 100 times. And you might appreciate the force of my argument by these examples. Sometimes, to avoid confusion, an entirely new word is simply made up to describe an object in the world. In the past, these have been cobbled together from the classical languages (like *telephone* and *linoleum*) probably to make them more immediately intelligible to 'well-educated' people. We can tell that we are using these new words correctly when we don't make mistakes with them - when our public use of them is meaningful. This has been likened to joining in a game with other people: everyone has to agree to abide by the rules of the game otherwise it gets spoilt. Games, and rules, can change but only if there is a lot of agreement (or little disagreement). Thus, though I object to *self-deprecate* substituting for *self-depreciate*, I fear I'm in too small a minority to stop this new 'rule' from continuing to spread. (And I have little hope of successfully introducing the term *pratbadge* for a car's registration number that has been specially selected with some whimsical or self-important motive.)

Where the 'language-rules' come from is debatable. There is strong evidence that our brains are natural language-generators and we are born to use language as naturally as we are born to grow longer arms. This has led to the claim that we are all born with the 'language-rules' wired into our brains. A counter-claim is that language conforms to certain rules which best 'infect' a young human brain as it encounters other people talking: the 'language-rules' lie outside the brain and in the language itself. Neither of these claims seem, to me anyway, to affect language as a vehicle for transmitting thought.

**What do sentences mean?**
Most of our language consists of sentences. In fact, once you get beyond the very young age when well-meaning people speak to you saying 'Spoon. Food. Dish. Mess' along with the appropriate gestures, nearly all of what is communicated is via sentences. After all these years at school you will be aware that it is when you are constructing sentences that the *rules of language* come into play; getting those cases, tenses, moods and agreements all sorted out is not so straightforward as it once was (when we learned our first language sitting in our high chair spattering mush about). But it has to be done, otherwise the sense of a sentence is lost or distorted. What language does is take words and use them in composition according to certain rules. These rules, when correctly applied, allow the sense of a sentence to be generated from the individual senses of the words in it. Of course, the words are important in themselves but in the end they are mere contributors to the meaning of the sentence. Once the sentence is uttered, heard or read, then the words become transparent to form a window that reveals a thought. This is especially evident when we use emotional language. The sentence "*She is gorgeous!*" uses words to convey the emotion of attraction to another human in an especially graphic way.

Generally, the thought we wish to communicate is a proposition that we intend to correspond to reality - we are passing something on that we believe to be true. (Unless we intend to lie.) The correspondence between our words and the real world is taken to make them meaningful. It is argued that meaningless sentences are ones that have no such correspondence.

It might be worthwhile to make a small digression at this point to deal with fiction. Since this is material that is not true, has it any meaning? Although we would all agree that Sherlock Holmes is not a part of the 'real' world, that does not stop us talking about him in a meaningful way. As a *fictional object which exists in the real world*, we can quite sensibly discuss his taste in music, attitude to women, sense of humour and so on. To be coherent in such discussions we just need to pay attention to Holmes' fictional world (so we cannot discuss his wife and children since he was unmarried) which itself pays attention to the real world (Holmes could not have gone jet-skiing after Moriarty, for instance, since he lived in Victorian England). Thus unreal things can be meaningful, and be associated with truth.

How do we know what a sentence means? Most would agree that we know what a sentence means when we understand what the author of the sentence *intends* it to mean. There are exceptions to this, especially in literature [see the section on Languages and Literature] but appreciating what the author intends is hugely problematical. The way we use words often depends on social convention. If someone asked me if I thought a particular hat suited them, my answer would depend on our relationship - especially if I thought it unsuitable. To someone close to me I could say '*Take it off, it's ghastly*' but to an acquaintance I might say '*I think a bolder style suits you better*'. My intention (to convey the thought that the hat is unsuitable) is the same in both cases but if you weren't aware of the convention then your interpretation may be 'wrong'. Thus we may be unable to disentangle meanings of some sentences from the acceptable etiquette between the communicators.

The *context* of the sentence is also critical. To take a simple example, what does the sentence "*She ate some of the cakes*" mean? This depends on how many cakes there were in the first place (the context). If there were 10 cakes we would assume that she had eaten some of them and left the others. But what it there were just two cakes originally? Now we would have to interpret the sentence as meaning that she ate a portion of one cake and a portion of the other. Or what if someone asked you if you knew anything about fish. You might answer "*I can't tell a sardine from a shark*" meaning that you know very little. One would assume that what you have said is not *literally* true (you actually *could* tell the difference between these two fish) but you have exaggerated to make the answer more striking. And sometimes the meaning can be conveyed by using an inappropriate sentence. What if you overheard the following between two fellow-students:

*"Is Mr Roberts a good teacher?"*
*"He wears very colourful ties."*

The meaning here is clear - the second student thinks Mr Roberts is not a good teacher - but the sentence is only about his ties!

Much of what is said and written *assumes a certain knowledge* in the listener/reader. If this assumption is wrong, then the meaning may be lost or distorted. And how can we make such a grand assumption given that we are all so different among ourselves, let alone among other groups in other places at other times?

**Thoughts and Words**
When I say something, my brain controls the messages sent to chest, voice-box, mouth, tongue and lips. Damaging parts of the brain impairs linguistic ability. These facts show that it is the brain that produces language. But how does it put a thought into words? And then how does your brain translate the words you hear into thoughts?

It might be that the brain actually talks to itself all the time and some of it we express, i.e. our thoughts are already in words. There certainly seems to be a sort of 'inner voice' that burbles on continuously in our heads, passing a running commentary on everything around us and in our memories. But if this is the case, what starts the burbling? It may be simply fed by sensory inputs 'Oh look, there is a dog biscuit. I wonder where Bonzo is? I hope he hasn't got wet because' and so on and on and on. But this implies that we have no control over our thoughts except, perhaps, in choosing the ones we express. (But even this, presumably, is initiated by a thought...)

Alternatively, we might envisage some 'creative centre' in the brain that inspires thoughts via some mental signals that are subsequently merely translated by the language-generating parts. This accounts for the way we can surprise ourselves by what we say. But it also puts our thoughts beyond our conscious control which is upsetting because don't we feel wholly in charge of what we are thinking about? And if we are not in charge of what we say, can we be in charge of what we mean?

The same problem arises in reverse when we hear or read something: how do we latch on to the thought that the words express? How do we 'read our own thoughts'?

These are problems of consciousness, I think, and fairly incidental to knowledge as it stands. It is almost self-evident that language works in its function of communicating thoughts from mind to mind. Nonetheless, it is easy to overlook that thinking is not as straight-forward as you might think.

# PART II
*Worlds of Knowledge*

# MATHEMATICS

*If two ride on a horse, one must ride behind.*

Mathematics is the most systematic form of knowledge that we have (especially when you consider that it embraces modern logic). By systematic, I mean that the methods used are rigid, rigorous and universal: once you have learnt the rules, and if you apply these rules correctly, then you will arrive at a conclusion that is identical with anyone else's. A mathematician is not satisfied with 'This might be the right answer' or 'Isn't it a pity that my right answer and your right answer to this question are not the same?' No, the mathematician can achieve *certainty* which, in a doubtful world, is a jewel without price. How can mathematicians be so sure of their knowledge?

**The nature of mathematical knowledge**
Although modern logic is mathematical in its scope and method, I have already dealt with logic's role in knowledge in the Reason section. What distinguishes mathematics from other areas of knowledge is that it is ultimately based on number and each branch of the subject uses the rules of inference that I discuss below. The separate branches, such as calculus and geometry, are based on different sets of axioms (though one in each set will refer to the algebra of numbers). Mathematics has its own system of notation (or language) that allows it to communicate mathematical knowledge clearly and precisely.

**a) Axioms**
An axiom is a fundamental statement that underpins the mathematics derived from it and is incapable of being derived itself. Generally, these axioms are 'self-evidently true'. An example of this from geometry is:

*If a, b, and c are points on a straight line, and b lies between a and c, then b also lies between c and a.'*

This is impossible to prove because we would need it to be true before we could start any proving process. Thus, we have to accept some things as true if we are to make any progress in knowledge at all. But the fewer these assumptions, and the more 'self-evident' they are, then the more confident we can be that our knowledge is secure. It is hard (impossible?) to imagine a world in which the axiom above could be false.

At first glance, setting out a few axioms that have the characteristics of self-evident truth seems fairly unpromising - how can simple truths lead to complex and surprising truths? No doubt your experience of mathematics has already furnished you with the answer to this question: very easily indeed! Euclid, for instance, started out with just 5 axioms and derived a bookful of proofs for plane geometry from them.

But basing one's knowledge on axioms might strike you as not being wholly satisfactory for two reasons. The first is that the self-evident truth is not really the same thing as the truth itself. It may be 'self-evident' to us but how can we be so sure that this is the case for everybody? The second is that an axiom might be quite arbitrary - made up by a mathematician because they have got nothing better to do. What about negative numbers, for example, or the square root of -1? Have such ideas got anything to do with the real world itself? Might the mathematics using such axioms exist only in mathematicians' minds? A robust reply might be: 'Who cares? Exploring the world of pure mathematics is as wonderful and fulfilling as exploring the fictions of Shakespeare and would anybody question that activity?'

Another reply is that, in fact, it *does* describe reality but that we don't appreciate it. If we look back into history there is some evidence to support this view. A straight-forward example comes from the mathematicians who decided to drop one of Euclid's 5 axioms, the one that had parallel lines meeting only at infinity. This led to the development of a geometry where parallel lines *can* meet and what sort of crazy world could this describe, you might ask? Well, the axioms can now give rise to a geometry that suits a sphere. The Earth is pretty close to being a sphere - all the lines of longitude, for instance, are parallel in that they all run north-south but they all meet at the north and south poles. Thus, although Euclid's plane geometry is 'correct', it is only correct for little bits of the world - the flat bits like the desktop, or a sheet of paper. A more 'realistic' world, we now see, comes from a set of axioms that appeared, at first, *not* to be an adequate description.

A second example comes from devising an axiom where 'imaginary numbers' (based on the square root of -1) produce another sort of mathematical world. This world, we now know, describes much of the electronics developed in the 20th century. So perhaps the world of the pure mathematician is the true world and maybe we need to be less downright about what we will accept as being 'real'. Just because you find it hard to imagine 10-dimensional space does not necessarily mean that there is no such a thing, does it?

Indeed, one of the valuable things about mathematics is that it can come up with surprising answers, ones that common sense will often reject. Consider a man who wants to row his boat upriver from A to B and immediately row back to A. If the river flows at 3kph, and the man can row steadily in still water at 6kph, and A and B are 6km apart, how long will he take? It is common sense (at least it is to me) to say that we can ignore the current of the river since he is going upriver for the same distance that he is going downriver - one will cancel out the other. Hence, after this simplification, the problem is really easy: he'll take an hour to go from A to B (6km at 6kph) and an hour to get back. Two hours in all. QED. It is a surprise to one's (my) common sense to discover this is wrong - he will, in fact, take 2 hours and 40 minutes.

The great strength of mathematics is that it can spell out how to arrive at the right answer by applying logical thinking rigorously -something that does not always come naturally to many of us.

There is a branch of mathematics that deals with the real world directly rather than the 'possible' or 'as yet, unrealised' world of, say, the mathematician in multi-dimensional space. This is called applied mathematics and it tries to produce equations that fit with what is experienced. This sort of mathematics is used, for instance, in forming models of how the weather behaves, or how epidemics spread, or how the stock markets fluctuate. The approach here is different in that it is not an exploration of the possibilities inherent in a set of axioms. The rules of mathematics are obeyed but the equations are adjusted to fit what is experienced. Often, the mathematician might start with 'ideal' conditions such as, in a weather model, the air moving uniformly, the Earth's surface being smooth, the rate of input of solar heat being constant, and so on. The predictions from this initial model are tested against reality and then modifications made. The new model is then checked, and this is repeated until the required level of accuracy is achieved. The answer is not 'right' just 'right enough'. A criticism of this approach is that it starts from an idealised model rather than the real world. And no such model can adequately capture the intricacies and complexities of this world. (This tendency to idealise the complex to make calculation simpler is lampooned in the story about the worried farmer who asked a mathematician what he would suggest that might help protect his herd of cows from BSE. The mathematician replies: 'Well, let's imagine your cows are spheres...')

**b) Rules of inference**
These are used to arrive at a mathematical proof - an argument that has no doubt about it (or as little doubt as we might reasonably expect). As with the axioms, we must just accept these as being self-evident but it would be difficult to challenge them - you've probably been using them unthinkingly all your mathematical life. There are

four main rules and here is one of them:

*At any stage in an argument we can substitute one statement by an equivalent statement.*

(Given that, say $a = b + 2$, this allows us, for example, to replace the equation *$2a - 3 = 3$* with *$2(b + 2) - 3 = 3$* and be sure that it is equivalent.)

As with the axioms, the rules of inference cannot be derived from anywhere else. We can just 'see' that they are right. This also applies to certain mathematical relationships - there is no need for us to check that $a \times b = b \times a$. All we need do is consider the area of a rectangle to see that it *must* be true.

Thus we might conclude that since we need have *no direct experience* of mathematical truths, and *cannot use reason* to arrive at the axioms and rules of inference, that mathematical knowledge lies beyond other sorts of knowledge in a world of its own.

**Are numbers real?**
As you might suspect, the answer to this question is not as simple as we might like. One group of thinkers believes that numbers (and, by implication, the rest of mathematics) describes a realm of objects that exist independently and so have a reality that is independent of our calculations and the real world. If this is the case, then we can 'tap into' this world by means of the proofs we discover. It is certainly the case that we have an inborn grasp of small numbers and simple arithmetical principles like subtraction and addition. Babies just a few months old know that $2 + 1 = 3$ or that $2 - 1 = 1$, for instance, as do other animals that have been tested such as dogs, dolphins, chickens and chimps. This is not to say that they *symbolise* quantities as in the sums above. What they recognise is that if you take one 'thing' away from two 'things' then just one 'thing' remains. They can do this only for small numbers of 'things'. Later in life, humans can drop the

'thing' part and just use the symbols, i.e; we come to know the world of numbers which exists independently of this 'real' world - where something like '3' is not anchored to any real object at all.

A second group of mathematical thinkers don't like the idea of a world containing strange objects like a number that stands only for itself, and where there are infinitely many of them. And how can mortal, physical humans get in touch with this separate world of numbers and mathematical relationships if the matter they are made of cannot affect the 'spirit' the numbers are made of? These people prefer to say that all we have is the concept of proof, and that mathematical theories extend only so far as the limits of mathematicians' brains. They would argue that babies, and other animals, do not know numbers as such, they just know about amounts of things, which is quite different. Going from 2 apples plus 2 bananas giving you 4 pieces of fruit, to *2 + 2 = 4* is a huge conceptual leap and not a small developmental step. People are only born with the sense of reason/logic which can be applied to the mathematical symbols and functions we create. This logical way of thinking, together with an innate grasp of the 'numerosity' of things that we share with other animals, is at the heart of our knowledge of mathematics.

If this second group is right, then mathematics is another human construct along the same lines as, say, science or art. Evidence in favour of this view is that mathematical knowledge, although it does progress, contains a past full of errors. Pure mathematicians have produced masses of theorems but only a minority has been fruitful. Thus, it might be argued that the only thing to recommend pure mathematical theories is that they have (near?) flawless internal consistency. But then again, good fairy stories also have flawless internal consistency (e.g. the wicked witch never does anything nice) and how believable are these? Applied mathematics, on the other hand, at least approximates to the real world (remember that it is not 'right', just 'right enough'). This good fit with reality relies on the accuracy of the observations on the real world itself - something discussed at greater length in the Natural Science section.

A third group of mathematicians banish even the idea of 'numerosity' as giving us an insight into the truth about the real world. They claim that all mathematics is based on purely arbitrary grounds and that mathematicians inhabit a fanciful world of their own creating. If they are right, then the subject becomes more of an art form where the artist-mathematician is constrained only by his materials and his imagination. This view does not appear to square with the fact that the real world (as we have discovered it through science) *does* exhibit mathematical relationships which we have also discovered (either by pure insight like the first group, or by trial-and-error like the second group).

One way to try to resolve these differences between mathematicians is to attempt to reduce all mathematics to the elementary laws of logic by avoiding numbers altogether. Towards the end of the 19th century, it was shown that all the basic ideas of arithmetic can be reduced to the theory of natural numbers; that numbers can be defined in terms of one-to-one correspondence; and that arithmetic can be reduced to a set of 5 axioms. These axioms contain just 3 undefined fundamental terms (*zero, number* and *successor*) but, despite much brilliance being expended, it was impossible to derive these from logic alone. Further, a mathematician has since proved that there can be *no* proof of the completeness of arithmetic which permits a proof of its consistency, and vice versa. It's like trying to bite your own teeth.

In sum, we are confident about the knowledge in mathematics because it is logical and can be recognised as such by anyone understanding the terms of the argument or proposition. It is a human activity that is creative and not just mechanical (your calculator is more accurate and faster than you at applying mathematical rules but is not a better mathematician). It also reflects at least some of the truths of the universe because we have discovered that the universe conforms to certain mathematical equations. Thanks to this mathematical knowledge, we are able to control our lives and world to a greater extent as well as to explore 'possible' worlds that may later be realised. The limitations of this knowledge, however, is that we have yet to discover (if this is possible) the mathematics that will give us equal certainty in what most of us might feel are the more immediately important areas of human concern - like: Where will I go? Who should I trust? What shall I do? Why is this so beautiful? When will you give me an answer?

# NATURAL SCIENCES

*Better a live dog than a dead lion.*

The natural sciences are generally regarded as being the best way yet for *generating* knowledge itself, albeit of a certain type. This type of knowledge is concerned with the physical, chemical, and biological parts of the world at a fairly basic level. Nonetheless, though the knowledge is basic, it has allowed humans to exercise a control over their environments that is unprecedented. Natural sciences achieve this power largely through searching for certainty, and demanding that any certainties established are reasonable, i.e. ones that all (reasonable) humans will acknowledge as objectively acceptable.

## The scope of the natural sciences

The natural sciences seek to explain what makes the real world work the way that it does. That there is a real world, independent of the human mind, is an assumption that most of us are ready to grant. That there are ways in which it works is not so readily granted: we wait for scientists to discover these ways, and then convince us that their discoveries are certain (or even true). We can all readily appreciate that the real world is a complex thing. Thus far, the natural sciences have tackled the ways that it works at the simplest level possible (though a glance at science text books shows that this by no means generates simple explanations). In future, they *may* be able to tackle more complicated levels such as the worlds of history, culture, ethics, and aesthetics. To see why this might be possible, we need to appreciate how science has worked so successfully in the past.

## Certainty and the natural sciences

We have seen in previous sections that we can arrive at certainty without referring to the real world at all. Thus, if we are certain that Fred is taller than Ben, and that Ben is taller than Tom, then Fred *must* be taller than Tom. There is no need for us to go and check whether this is the case. In a similar way, the proofs derived in mathematics are certain. What distinguishes the scientific certainties from those of logic and maths is that they use data that comes from observation of the real world. This does not mean that they are necessarily any less certain. But what it does mean is that they are more open to doubt.

What I've just written may appear meaningless but perhaps what follows will make it clearer. It is certain that one individual pencil cannot be two individual pencils at the same time. Of this, there is no doubt at all - because it is *logically impossible*. It is also certain that if you stopped eating you would die. I dare say that you are as certain of this as nearly anything. However, we might still regard it as being open to doubt because we can *imagine* that it is possible for someone not to eat and yet not die (like, say, someone with an amazingly low metabolic rate who lies comatose for years on end before dying of 'natural causes' other than starvation). Being open to doubt is the price that natural sciences pay in order to make progress. Thus, while it is *logically* possible to build a ladder to the Moon, the natural sciences tell us that it is *physically* impossible to do so and find us an alternative way of getting there. The reason why a ladder wouldn't work, and the reason why rockets *do* work, is to do with the laws of nature.

**Laws of Nature**
We assume that the real world exists. We further assume that the behaviour of the real world is constrained by laws. (It is hard to imagine how a world without any laws could exist at all, since even existing obeys the law of existence.) Everything that the natural sciences embrace relies on uncovering these laws of nature. Once we know the laws of nature then we are in a position to predict the future and hence to give ourselves real choices about what happens. How do scientists go about finding the laws of nature? How are they so sure that they have found them?

## a) Finding the laws

The simplest way of finding a law would seem to be: Watch something that keeps happening, and, if it always happens the same way, then that's the law. Thus, if the arrival of Saturday has always been accompanied by rain then you have discovered the law that it always rains on Saturdays. Once you know the law you can confidently carry your umbrella every Saturday knowing that you will need it. The main problem with this approach is that the past has not been a reliable guide to the future. We can't be sure whether what we have been watching has been either a coincidence, or not *directly* connected to an outcome.

Coincidence may be ruled unlikely if you watch enough pairs of events that you thought were connected. But could you ever be *certain* that this pair of events were definitely not coincidental in the same way as you are *certain* that *2 + 2 = 4*? There would always be a doubt, even if it was negligible.

And what if what you were watching was not *directly connected* to the outcome? Say you were looking at an electric iron to see how it works and you observe that whenever the iron is getting hotter, a red light comes on. You may well think the law is that the red light makes the iron get hotter (or that the iron getting hotter makes the red light come on). However, I'm sure you know that the red light has nothing directly to do with the heating of the iron: it's just an indicator and hence your 'law' (either of them) is false.

One way of getting round the problem of assuming that the future is like the past is to find out the *cause* of how the outcome is related to the starting conditions. This is a very important aspect of the natural sciences. When it looks as though there is a relationship of cause and effect (like the 'cause' of Saturday producing the 'effect' of rain; or the 'cause' of the red light producing the 'effect' of a hotter iron), a scientist will start searching for the best explanation available to account for it. The 'explanation' they come up with is called a hypothesis. There are no rules for making up hypotheses but scientists will usually start with ones that don't break any of the known laws of nature or are not contradicted by existing evidence. (This is not to say that hypotheses that ignore these are wrong. Some outstanding advances have been made in science by people ignoring 'laws' and 'facts' of the past. That said, such advances that have been achieved in this way are very few, and very far between.) Coming up with hypotheses to explain cause and effect relationships is a very creative and imaginative process. As with other creative aspects of human thinking, 'rules' that could produce such thought seem to be a contradiction in terms. (Except, perhaps, the rule: Ignore all rules.)

If possible, scientists will then test their hypothesis by experiment to check whether it works or not. (I will return to experimentation later.) If it *does* work then it is called a theory or, if it works really convincingly, a law. Thus we are less sure that everything in the universe is based on atoms (atomic theory) than that the universe is getting more disorderly overall (second law of thermo-dynamics.)

### b) Being sure of the laws

What gives scientists the confidence that their laws are the same as those laws that dictate the behaviour of the real world? There are some thinkers about science who deny that we can ever know any such thing. They say that the laws and theories put forward contain things which we cannot observe and hence cannot verify. As an example, take the theory that matter is made up of atoms. These cannot be observed without building a machine which is designed to 'see' them as scientists expect them to be. This is like looking for red things with a red-thing detector which we have programmed to respond to things we think are red. In fact, there may be no red things at all but the machine may quite reliably 'detect' things we thought should be red. Such thinkers say that the laws and theories are convenient fictions that help us get along, but that there is no way of knowing if they are near the truth or not. They argue that we should *never* believe in such laws and theories because there is *never* enough evidence to be convincing.

Other thinkers are less plagued by doubt. One feature of science that gives them more confidence is that our explanations tie in together so well and have got to more fundamental levels. Thus, though the law used to calculate the gravitational force between bodies is ideal (i.e. it exists only as an idea since it assumes no other forces are acting at the same time - which is impossible), it also helps explain the science behind the behaviour of falling bodies and planetary motion. The coherence of this network of scientific laws, and its robustness given new discoveries, gives these scientists greater confidence and certainty that they are describing the Universe as it really is.

A second feature that gives confidence is when laws are put on a quantitative basis. When we use mathematics to describe the behaviour of the world we gain a precision in prediction that is far easier to test and measure. This relies on the confidence we have in mathematics and its methods which, as I set out in the previous section, can be claimed to be among the strongest we might reasonably hope for.

Another feature of science that produces more confidence in its getting nearer the truth is the way that scientists go about their business, the way they employ *reliable methods* in their work. It is generally agreed that there is no single scientific method. Rather, there is a whole spectrum of approaches from the very general '*Try to prove your hypothesis wrong*' to the very specific '*Test it with litmus paper to see if it really is acidic*'. What these methods have in common is that they have proved reliable in the past as a means for generating knowledge. Not only that, such methods do not rely on the mind of the individual. In other words, the methods are objective - and can be seen to be reliable by everyone who cares to look. Thus, although we cannot rule out *any* method for examining scientific theories and laws, we can be more confident in using t-tests rather than tea leaves to predict the future because the former have proved more reliable than the latter.

I expect you will have noticed that such scientists' dependence on reliable methods is open to the same objection as devising laws and theories in the first place: they have worked in the past but why should they work in the future? An answer to this is that our explanations have got fewer, but more powerful, as time has passed. This carries a strong implication that we are near (if not at) the truth. That, for example, matter really *is* made up of atoms. Against this, why *should* the Universe be subject to simple and powerful laws? There doesn't seem to be an answer to this beyond pointing to past success in using these criteria.

**Observing**
Scientists make observations and when they do this they are open to the objections that I've rehearsed in the 'Perception' section. More to the point, before they start making any observations at all, they have an expectation in mind. No scientist simply makes observations - feverishly writing down everything going on around them. No, they observe things they *expect to be relevant*. Thus, when observing something involving electricity, the scientist will pay attention to the current, resistance, voltage, and so on, without paying attention to the colour of their socks or the size of the room. In other words, the scientist already has a theory in mind before starting to check a little bit of the world to see if the theory has any merit. This could mean that they might miss something that really is important, or that they might be biased in that they are looking for evidence that will confirm their idea and not evidence that will 'spoil' it.


**Experimenting**
Many of us associate science with experimentation: devising, carrying out and then interpreting a test of a hypothesis. The process we learn for laboratory work is generally the 'controlled experiment'. This depends on a piece of logical thinking that goes along the lines of: If events A, B, C lead to event D, assume that one or more of A, B, C, *causes* D. Then, test to see if you can get the result D by using first A by itself; then B by itself; then C by itself. If only one of them

(e.g. B) gives the result D, then say 'B causes D'. (If none of them work individually you have to try the various combinations until it works.)

For this technique to work, then in each experiment we need to keep everything that might influence the outcome, D, exactly the same except just one thing (in turn, A, then B, then C). The first problem is that this is impossible: we cannot keep everything exactly the same. Time and the positions of the stars, for instance, will never be the same for two experiments.

A second problem is that to carry out such experimental work involves practical skill in mastering the technique and competence in handling novel equipment. Because this requires a little talent and some practice, the results initially, or those produced by someone new to it, will often not agree with the theory. Thus, experienced experimenters will often discard 'faulty' results on the grounds that the likelihood of their being correct is less than that of the theory being tested being incorrect. A sceptic could object that experimenters are just throwing away perfectly good data simply because it is contradictory. This is why scientists set great store on experiments being *repeatable*: if there really *were* a relationship between the cause B and the effect D then it should work time after time no matter who performs the experiment.

Laboratory experiments are not the only sort of testing scientists do. In drug-testing, for example, it is clearly impossible to get two groups of people who are identical in *every* respect except that one group is given a drug and the other a harmless substitute. Here, scientists use what they call 'random sampling' and statistical techniques to produce probabilities of the efficacy of the drug. Can one get a sample of people that is truly random? This is extremely difficult to achieve without knowing everything about all the people under test. And the statistical techniques used generally start out with the assumption that the probability of a link between the cause and effect is zero and can be accounted for by chance alone. This is supposed to eliminate subjective bias. However, the level at which this assumption is rejected in favour of a non-random explanation is arbitrary, and has led to contradictory claims in many areas - examples include passive smoking causing lung cancer; red wine being good for you; power lines causing cancer. If scientists agree that the methods and techniques they have used are correct and yet their conclusions are contradictory, what value can we place on their claims?

Laboratory experiments are not possible when it comes to investigating some scientific areas. In cosmology we cannot experiment on the 'big bang'; in geology we cannot fiddle with plate tectonics; in biology we cannot re-run time to see if dinosaurs will evolve into birds again. Here it is possible to make observations that fit with the theory and to check the predictions that flow from the theories, such as universal background radiation; changes in distances between continents; comparative anatomy. When observation confirms prediction scientists have greater confidence in such theories.

**Progress**
Most of us would agree that science has made progress in that the knowledge we have now is greater and more profound than in the past. In this respect, today's science is better than that of the previous century. This progress is like that in mathematics: it builds on what has gone before. (Note that such progress is not claimed elsewhere. In the world of literature, for instance, most of us wouldn't claim that modern writers have progressed beyond Shakespeare or Homer and thus are better.) This idea has been challenged on the grounds that the history of science can be seen as the supplanting of an old theory by a quite different new one. An example is the adoption of the theory that the Sun is at the centre of the solar system rather than the Earth. How can we *know* that the new theory is better and not just different? The answer usually given is that the new theory is a better explanation because not only does it account for the data in the old theory, but it also explains features that the old theory couldn't, and makes novel

predictions that open up new areas of science to be explored. Often, it also strengthens or unifies other scientific theories that were perhaps seen as lying in different fields.

Thus, in its own terms, science can legitimately claim to have made progress. However, when we come to the *application* of science that is quite another matter. The scientific advances in nuclear power, chemical pesticides and genetic engineering, for instance, are unquestionable: all are extensions of our knowledge. However, many would dispute that this knowledge is 'good'. But such arguments lead us away from the world of science and into the worlds of ethics and social responsibility. Worlds where the certainties of science seem to have little of value to contribute.

# HUMAN SCIENCES

*A cat in gloves catches no mice.*

Human sciences is a broad category that includes all subjects in which the behaviour of humans in a social context plays a part. The aim of the human sciences is to explain the patterns of behaviour that we see among people. The underlying aim is to be able to use any explanations for the greater good of humanity in the future.

It is hard to think of humans outside a social structure. Indeed, it might be argued that without society you cease to be properly human at all. There are a few tragic examples of young children who were brought up by other animals who behave like those animals rather than like humans. And some adults have abandoned social interactions by living as hermits - but such people are usually regarded as being either psychologically disturbed or divinely inspired. In either case, you might not see them as 'normal'.

For humans, living and interacting with other humans seems to be a part of our nature. These interactions work on many levels: the one-to-one of, for instance, boyfriend and girlfriend; the family group; the circle of friends; the community at school; a social grouping (such as race, class, religion); nationality; and affinity for all others in the human species on Earth. The spectrum is broad.

What separates human from natural sciences is the involvement of minds *in the process being observed*. Some natural scientists quite legitimately investigate the minds of individuals. What human scientists investigate are the products of the interactions of minds in social settings. Minds are extraordinarily complex things even by themselves. But when you put two or more of them together you get some wonderful and fascinating results. What do human scientists do to gain their insights into our social world? Where does their knowledge come from?

## Acquiring knowledge

The methods used by the natural sciences, especially the physical sciences, have proved to be a powerful way of arriving at explanations of the natural world. Since human beings may be taken to be just another part of this natural world, it would seem sensible to apply the methods of science to the social behaviour of humans. This is acknowledged in the term 'sciences' in the categorization. The scientific approaches to gaining knowledge that are shared by the human sciences are:

a) being objective (the thoughts of the person doing the studying should make no difference to the facts reported).
b) being open to constructive criticism (other human scientists review the facts and interpretations reported seeking out strengths and flaws and this adds something to the body of knowledge).
c) using observation as the principle means of acquiring facts.

One major difference is that the *experiment* is largely absent from human sciences. One reason for this is ethical - most of us would agree that experimenting on humans is unacceptable. A second reason is that a 'scientific' experiment is impossible to perform. This is because there is no such thing as a 'standard' human mind in the same way as there are standard atoms, metals and hearts. Our minds are all unique and so we will behave in a way that is peculiar to us as individuals. A third reason is that it is inappropriate - would we expect an explanation of why humans enjoy parties to be similar in any way to an explanation of why water flows downhill?

Later these 'reasons' will be challenged but for now let's turn to how human scientists get down to the nitty-gritty of acquiring facts about us.

## Observation

To get any information about how people behave socially we have to watch what they do, or what they have done, and note the outcomes. Thus, human scientists go out into the real world and make their observations and collect information. These observations may lead to information being quantitative or qualitative. A simple *quantitative* example would be an extra ten thousand tins of dog-food that were sold after an advertising campaign using 50 posters. A simple *qualitative* example would be to gauge people's response to the dog-food posters by asking them if they thought they were "*a) very good, b) quite good, c) poor, or d) very bad*". Both sorts of information are useful but in different ways.

In the first case we are trying to take the human minds out of the equation by just concentrating on what they actually do rather than what they think. All the dog-food buyers will be different but these differences are not important to us here. We can eliminate the differences and get a numerical link between posters and extra tins sold. This looks like good, hard, scientific data.

In the second case we are acknowledging that things are not so simple. Some people might have bought the extra tins for other reasons that have nothing to do with the posters. They might not even have seen the posters. Showing them the posters directly and asking people what they think gives us a good reason for judging their effectiveness.

Of course, it would be a naive dog-food manufacturer who relied exclusively on either sort of information. But without facts acquired in ways such as these it is hard to see how something like a business enterprise could be sustained. From a ToK point of view, however, we would ask how certain we can be that these are facts at all.

## The problems of 'factual' information in human sciences

Let's take the quantitative information first. This sort of information is valued because of the certainty that comes from applications of mathematical methods which rely on the logic of quantities and relationships between them. Also, as in the natural sciences, once we have a relationship established between objects in the real world, we can make predictions about what will happen in the future. This leads to human scientists claiming that there are principles, and even laws, which govern certain social interactions - like the *law of diminishing returns* in economics, for example. The assumption in this gathering of numerical data is that the humans being observed are basically the same: they can be reduced to a number for the purposes of measuring a particular piece of behaviour. We can pare away all the aspects of human minds that make them unique to leave a core that all human minds share. This seems reasonable doesn't it? After all, if we didn't have similar minds we would be unintelligible to each other. We must have similar minds because we are in the same species. We must have similar minds because we have been brought up in similar ways in similar societies. But is this wholly convincing?

To return to our posters and dog-food example, we could say that five posters lead to 1000 extra tins of dog-food sold, i.e. 1 poster leads to 200 extra tins sold. Would you be convinced that by putting up 5 000 posters you would sell 1 million extra tins? Probably not. You would want to modify the simple equation to take account of other factors - where the posters are placed, the information in the poster, the colours used in it, the cost of production, how the qualities of your dog-food are already perceived, the type of dog-owner you are targeting, the activities of your competitors, the financial situation in the country generally, and so on. Could all of these be put into numbers and then fed into the equation? Probably not.

This is not to say that it is of no value to *try* to do this. It does, however, illustrate the difficulty of the numerical approach. This difficulty is further exemplified by the generally poor predictive power of equations produced by human scientists. But, like weather-forecasting, as more information is gathered and our equations are revised and modified, we may get better at forecasting what is complex in the future. At least we could argue that history has shown that this method has worked for complex things in the past and so is a reliable approach so far as it goes.

The use of statistical methods is widespread in the human sciences. The equations here are designed to account for chance - both the chance that the quantity you are sampling is representative of the infinite whole; and the chance that the effect you see does not have the cause you expected (i.e. that it is random). Both of these are open to question. Are *you* a perfect representative of your school? If we got 20 of you and found some averages, would we *then* have a perfect representative of your school? We might be a bit closer. Of course, we might then question whether a perfect representation of your school really exists. And even if it did, would it be the same for the pupils, teachers, parents, outsiders? Hence, sampling might well not give you the most representative picture. Also, the effect you see may be just a random one. Statistics will give you some sort of *probability* that one thing has caused another. This lack of certainty is the price you have to pay to get very far quantitatively in the human sciences. Statistics will not remove a question mark, only make it smaller.

What about qualitative information? Here we run into the problem of people telling the truth. When people respond to a questionnaire, or are surveyed, the assumption is that they will give an honest answer. But are people always honest in the sense that they will give you truthful answer to what you ask? This depends on what your question is, how other people might answer the question, and what relationship you have to the person asking the question. Just reflect on what your answer might be to the question "*Will you come with me to see 'Hamlet'*" if you were a girl and the questioner were: a) your English teacher, b) your brother, c) a girlfriend, or d) a prospective boyfriend. Your reply would have something to do with your wanting to see the play but would also have other things to do with the relationship itself - to impress with your keenness as a student, or give family support, or as an act of friendship or because it shows amiable commitment. It is difficult - some might say impossible - to disregard the rest of humanity when answering a question. We wish people to see us as we want to be seen. Not only that, we wish different people to see us in different lights. If we answer '*yes*' to going to see *Hamlet*, we want the person asking us to understand our reply in terms of the relationship.

People might answer your questions to appear polite or to fit in with what they think you want to hear. Earlier this century, an anthropologist reported on the free sexual lifestyle of a group of Pacific islanders. As you can imagine, this got lots of publicity. Later, it turned out that the Pacific island teenagers were telling her fibs - she seemed so keen to talk about sexual matters that they entertained her with lots of lurid (fictitious) details about themselves to make her happy.

To get round this problem we can try to make the relationship as impersonal as possible. One way would be to pose the question on paper and say that responses will remain anonymous. This might seem to be the best way to get objective information. But are people capable of being honest even with themselves? Let's go back to our tins of dog-food. In the interests of getting objective information, we send a print of a poster to someone and ask them to give it a rating in terms of it being '*very good*', '*quite good*' and so on. Well, if it were sent to me, my first question would be: "'*Very good*' in what way?" Do they mean artistically? Or how well the information is spelt out? Or how well-produced it is? Or whether the dog-food sounds better? Or whether it makes sense financially? It would certainly make a difference if I owned a dog; or if my friend had recommended an alternative brand, or if I were rich enough not to care about the cost. Could all these very personal considerations be accounted for in a questionnaire? If not, wouldn't this devalue the responses that are made? Might I not want to appear discerning, thoughtful and intelligent in my reply rather than as someone going for the cheapest way to keep my dog well-fed?

One further problem is that we might not be truthful even with ourselves. Some people believe that we have subconscious desires over which we have no control. For example, we might subconsciously yearn to be like our parents which is why, to the outsider, we behave like them, while all the time we would vigorously deny any resemblance to them at all. If this idea about the subconscious is so, then we don't even know ourselves whether we are 'really' telling the truth or not.

In short, can we take other people at 'face-value'? Don't we always see them at their own *projected* face value? And isn't that projected face-value at some variance with the *true* value? If so, how reliable is their evidence?

Thus, when it comes to the 'facts' of human sciences, we might suspect the numbers because they miss out the human element and we might suspect the human element because it has proved an unreliable witness.

### The problem of the objective observer
In all of the above we were assuming that at least *we* were capable of noting down the responses of other people without any bias. But how true is this? Let's try one of the best-loved approaches to this question, the *thought-experiment*. (This is where, in our minds alone, we follow through the consequences of a given set of circumstances to try to clarify some idea or other.) Let's imagine that you are transported deep into a rain-forest and discover a previously unknown tribe of humans. Given that you have a keen and humane intellect, you will be curious as to how this novel human society works. What do you do?

Your first thought might be to remain hidden and observe them without interference of any kind. The trouble with this is that your interpretations of the activities that go on might be quite wrong and you wouldn't be aware of it. An example of this comes from anthropologists who reported on what a certain African tribe regarded as important when deciding where to camp. They observed that the Africans spent most time discussing the spiritual significance of one site rather than another and concluded that this must be the crucial factor. This seems a reasonable conclusion to draw. They were wrong, however. The factors that the tribe *did* consider as crucial, such as the availability of food and water at one site rather than another, were so obvious that they merited little discussion. It was only when they were down to the fine details of alternative campsites that relatively minor considerations, like what the spirits might prefer, were debated. (In the same way, a visitor from outer space might observe humans and conclude, on the basis of the time we spend discussing them, that hairstyles, holiday destinations and TV soaps are of greater importance to us than politics, science and literature.)

Aware of this, you reluctantly introduce yourself to the tribe. Your reluctance, of course, stems from the knowledge that your presence might well influence their 'natural' behaviour. (Much as a the presence of a visitor from outer space might affect the way you behave while it was watching you.) Anyway, you settle in and start making your notes. But what sorts of things will you make notes on? This is where bias is perhaps inevitable. If you're like me, you would think that births, marriages, deaths, the rituals of eating and drinking, religious observance, ways of educating the young, the place of elders in the society, and so on, will all be important. But that is simply because they are important to us. I might totally disregard something the tribe *does* regard as important simply through my ignorance - my ignorance of what it is like to be a part of the tribe itself.

So let's take the thought-experiment even further. Let's imagine that you have so immersed yourself in their ways and culture that you are fully accepted as a member of the tribe. You learn their language, take part in all the rituals, believe all the beliefs, behave in a way that is identical to any other member of the tribe. Surely *now* you can be objective about why they behave as they do? Well ... no. Because, if *that* were true, each of us could be objective about the tribe we *do* belong to at the moment, and give wholly impartial, honest answers to things people ask us about our behaviour in questionnaires about dog-food, for example. And as we've seen, we can't be trusted to be totally reliable witnesses.

It seems that objectivity about human behaviour is doomed to failure: objectivity would be possible only if we were not human; and if we were not human we wouldn't be able to interpret our own behaviour.

**Some counter-arguments**
*"Let's leave thought-experiments behind and get back to the real world,"* a pragmatic human scientist might say. Firstly, we *can* do experiments on people and gain reliable information just as in the natural sciences - especially the non-physical sciences like biology. Experiments on people are not unethical if the people are sane adults who have volunteered and if those experiments involve no cruelty. Psychologists routinely carry out such experiments and have clarified a number of our behavioural responses in certain social contexts.

Secondly, human nature is something that we *all* share. Part of that nature is our behaviour. Finding out about the biochemistry of our cells is applicable from one human to another and, in just the same way, finding out about social behaviour is applicable from one human to another. It's just more difficult to do, that's all. But if we keep working at it then, like biochemistry, it will start to yield the truth and we will be able to be more confident about the reasons for human behaviour. Then we can build on this knowledge and make society better for all.

Thirdly, it is *entirely* appropriate to look for relationships between humans as we look for relationships between non-human physical objects. There are causal laws which govern the latter - the laws of nature that we have discovered. Why should we human physical objects be any different? Aren't there laws of human nature that are yet to be discovered?

Lastly, though we might not be capable of objectivity as individuals, the society of human scientists is capable of objectivity as a whole because we are a diverse group and constructively criticise all that our members produce. We can be confident that we are aiming at, and getting nearer to, the truth about human social behaviour because we know more about it now than we did 50 years ago: What we are doing works.

# HISTORY

*The higher a monkey climbs, the more of his tail-end he shows.*

History deserves separate treatment from the others grouped in the Human Sciences section. The reason for this is that it forms a part of *all* other areas of knowledge - every subject has a history which, to some extent, influences how knowledge is currently gained and developed. Thus, the aims and methods used in history are bound to have implications for those subjects' claims to knowledge.

**What historians do**
Most of us think of historians as being people who give us a reliable account of the past. In part, this is true: one aspect of the job is to attempt to establish accurately such things as the dates of kings and the winners of battles; we want to know when Eric Bloodaxe ruled and who won at Borodino. These historical facts are relatively easy to come by. But such facts by themselves are not history, they are chronology - a setting down of the dates when things happened. What historians do is take such facts and then add *meaning*. In other words, they add in the human element.

**Evidence**
If you were to die tomorrow, what evidence would you leave behind? No doubt, like the rest of us, you exist as a name and number in various government records. Other institutions, like schools and clubs, will have evidence of some aspects of your life. There will be your clothes and other belongings. There may be photographs, letters, postcards. Perhaps you will have kept a diary, written stories about yourself. There will be memories of you in the minds of the people who knew you. Of these bits of evidence about you, which will survive? The answer from history is that it is the *recorded* evidence that counts. Unless recorded in some way (usually in writing) your feel-

ings, attitudes, intentions, desires, hopes, fears and so on will all disappear with you. But these are the things that give a meaning to the facts of your life - why you were laughing in this photograph, why you left that particular school.

(We generally regard *oral* history as somehow more suspect than written history perhaps because of the fluidity and flexibility of language, as well as the passing of 'facts' through many minds, rather than just one. Minds are not good at perfect reproduction of complex facts, stories and so on. But oral history will *at least* add colour to a picture of the past.)

Given this bias towards preservation of only certain types of material about the past - written records - then the first problem for the historian is that there is only partial evidence to go on. Unrecorded material is lost forever.

The second problem, related to the first, is that those people and societies that did not keep recorded evidence have not much of a place in history. History is inevitably biased towards the literate. Not only that, the people keeping records were usually rich, powerful, old and male (or employed by such). Almost inevitably, these people wrote about themselves and their peers. Consequently there is less material for the historian when dealing with the poor, the powerless, the young and females.

The third problem is that the evidence that *does* survive is often selective. The Romans left about 10 million words in Latin. Of these, about 2 million are to do with the law because lawyers thought them worth preserving. The UK government produces about 100 miles of records annually but only 1 mile is preserved because there is too little space for all of it.

The fourth problem is whether the evidence left is accurate or not. Evidence is recorded by humans and it is argued that humans cannot be objective - our account will always contain bias of some sort or another. Sometimes the history is written to flatter a ruler or patron. Sometimes the history is distorted to put the leaders of society in a better light (or opponents in a worse one). Sometimes the truth is suppressed out of fear of consequences. It is because of this last consideration that many historians decried the British government's decision in the 1960s to change the period for which official papers were kept secret before being made public. Such papers were previously kept for 50 years before being released. This period was reduced to 30 years. On the face of it, this looks like a good thing for history - a more accurate account of what the government's objectives and actions were at the time means a more accurate assessment of modern events. But many historians argued that the people in government would be less likely to keep truthful or full records because those same people would probably still be alive when the records were released (and so liable to be called to account) - unlike under the old 50-year rule. Thus the records for future historians of the UK *may* contain more omissions and distortions than would previously have been the case.

Finally, the evidence has to be approved of when judged against *non-historical* standards. Take witch-craft as an example. There is ample historical evidence that witches existed in the past: a massive amount of written records; eye-witness accounts; sworn testimony before the law; a rich literature in which they figure; near-universal belief among the best-educated; little variation in the belief over a long period. But, despite all this, most people today would dismiss such evidence because it doesn't fit in with our modern 'scientific' outlook.

**Putting the meaning into history**

Once historians have got the evidence, what do they do? That depends on the historian. Some believe all the evidence; some treat the evidence as nothing more than propaganda; some say that the evidence tells us *something* about the people and events. But what all historians do is try to *account* for the events of history. They look for the motives behind the human behaviour that produces historical events. It is for this reason that history can be endlessly re-interpreted: a student can produce a fresh insight into what has happened, one which the 'experts' have overlooked or not appreciated. But how do we get at the motives that drive other humans to do one thing rather than another?

One way a historian might do this is through empathy - by imagining themselves in the position of people in a particular historical period. This acknowledges that there is no point in even trying to be objective about history because everyone carries a load of cultural baggage from modern times. (It also requires that the historian be steeped in *all* the various factors that might influence human behaviour in that period since any of them could be of importance.)

The criticisms of this approach are four-fold. The first is that people cannot fully empathise even with a *contemporary* human being (could you confidently say what the precise motives of any other living human being are?) let alone someone from a different historical period. Secondly, public figures are adept at disguising their true motives so how can anyone be confident they have shared the 'true', rather than the professed, motives? Thirdly, people cannot dispassionately step from their mind into someone else's; they will always have their own thoughts colouring their interpretation. Fourthly, verification of an interpretation is impossible. The interpretation that one person has derived cannot be claimed to be nearer than anyone else's. There is no way to choose between the different interpretations, each is equally valid: there is no such thing as an authority.

An alternative approach is to say that, certainly, empathy has a place in the interpretation of history, but only a small place. It's importance is easily over-rated. What is of greater significance is that there *is* a mass of objective evidence from the past and much of it is coherent (containing no contradictions). Also, human nature is much the same as it ever was and we can use this in producing plausible and reasonable explanations of the way people have behaved that has led not just to 'grand' historical events such as battles and treaties, but also to social attitudes to such things as divorce and suicide. We can apply the models from current sociological and economic thinking to periods from the past and fruitfully explore any new light they shed on events there because such models have a proven capacity for accuracy. If we accept this approach, then we would show a greater regard for the conclusions of an 'expert' historian rather than a tyro: authority rules.

## Causes in history

What caused the First World War? Before we look at the ways to answer this question perhaps we ought to deal with the word 'cause'. In science we have cause and effect - striking a ball causes it to move a certain distance. One thing follows from the other. If we struck the ball in the same way again (and all other things were the same) then it would move the same distance. We don't have that same sort of predictability and replicability in history so 'cause' here has a less rigorous meaning. 'Explanation' may be a better term for the historical 'cause'.

Back to the War. When I was at school I remember being told that what caused the War was the shooting of Archduke Franz Ferdinand in Sarajevo. This prompts the question: if the student who fired the gun had missed, would there have been a War at all?

Some would say not. Since all events have causes, they say, we can trace great events back through chains of causes and so identify what triggers them. If you altered even one of these, then history would follow a different course.

Others disagree. They say that it is silly to look for causes of great events in minute historical details. Great events have rules of their own which follow patterns that are not capable of being reduced to small things - much as looking at the behaviour of the individual water molecules in the sea is not going to inform you of the behaviour of the tidal wave moving across it.

We would like to be sure of the causes of historical events because it might help us avoid repeating some of the nastier bits of human behaviour or even help to increase the number of the nicer bits. Given what has been said above, this seems to be beyond our grasp at present. (Few modern historians seem to be able to take current events and accurately predict what will happen.) However, an optimist might point to the fact that the behaviour of individuals in the past is still intelligible to us; that human nature has not changed much and so won't change much. And they might point to the interpretation of great events as having rules of their own and say we should devote our energies to looking for these rules. This would give the chance for historians to contribute rather more to the world of ideas than has yet been the case. (There are very few theories about the past.) One might hope that, in the future, we will have the knowledge to apply history for the greater good.

# LANGUAGES AND LITERATURE

*A sow may whistle though it has an ill mouth for it.*

In Part I, in the section on Language and Meaning, I looked at how our knowledge is framed and transmitted by way of words and sentences and how language is crucial to the clarification and expression of thought. In this section I want to look at two areas that stem from this: knowledge in languages other than verbal ones; how literature can use words to transcend language and what sort of knowledge this consists in.

**Nonverbal languages**
I am going to say nothing here about what is loosely called 'body language' although this isn't to say it is not an important means of communication. My reason for omitting it is because the persons involved are unconscious of the knowledge being transmitted. It becomes knowledge only when people talk and write about it - in other words, when it is transmitted verbally. Without having it explained to you, you don't 'know' that raising your head might indicate assertiveness any more than you 'know' you sweat to cool down. The 'knowledge' is automatic and unthinking. In this respect we are just like other animals, and the knowledge we deal with in ToK is not the sort of knowledge that, say, a dog has.

I shall also pass over conventions and codes such the Western tradition of wearing black to indicate mourning for the dead, or medals to indicate service or bravery in conflict. These are more interesting in that they reflect cultural differences and attitudes as well as transmitting information about the probable state and status of other people. That said, they are a very limited sort of communication more akin to the hoot of the chimpanzee than language proper.

The symbols used in arithmetic have the characteristic that they are unambiguous. Once you have grasped the concepts of '2', '+' and '=' then the statement that '2 + 2 = 4' can have *only one meaning*. This is what is at the heart of the language of arithmetic. It is not that the symbols are simply a convenient shorthand for words, it is that the symbols are absolutely precise in the way that words usually are not. This reflects the certainty that lies in this area of knowledge. Here clarity and precision are paramount and the use of these symbols guarantees that anyone who understands the symbols can follow the reckoning. Thus it is a language that can be used by anyone in the world with the certainty that anyone else will agree with your arithmetic (provided you make no mistake in applying the rules).

A short step from these symbols are the ones used in formal logic and some of those in mathematics. These do stand for words but the words themselves are deemed to have only one meaning. Thus the symbol for *integrate* (and the word itself) has just one meaning in mathematics and the symbol ¬ means "it is not the case that" in logic. Again, these allow for certainty to be preserved and communicated. The problem with the artificial languages that are used in logical analysis, is that they can only *approximate* to natural languages like English or Mandarin. They are very effective when any ambiguity is absent and the context is clear. Unfortunately, much of what is spoken or written is difficult to fit into an artificial language exactly. Even as simple a word as 'a' can prove intractable. Consider what it means in this sentence:

*There are just 5 natural kingdoms in biological systematics: animals, plants, fungi, bacteria, and protoctists, and Green has written a book on all of them.*

How many books has Green written here, five or one? If we had no way of checking, we couldn't know.

Musical notation is another form of language and there are some

*Languages and Literature*

people who will read a musical score on the train as you or I might read a short story. What sort of knowledge does music convey and how does the language permit or constrain it? We can put most musical knowledge under the umbrella term of aesthetics but might add that other types of music serve different ends - like the clarion-call insistence of the signature tune announcing that The News has arrived on television, or the 'muzak' of the shopping mall. More serious music, generally called classical music, aims at an *intellectual* engagement with the listener. This intellectual area, like other areas such as science and history, needs development if classical music is to be appreciated. Some of this development can be undertaken verbally but you also need to listen to the music. At first sight you might think that musical symbolism allows the precision of, say, maths. The notes indicate the sound to be made, for how long and in what order. Other symbols indicate the volume and style and so on. And yet precision is not all that a piece of music is about; one could program a computer to play a symphony with absolute authenticity and no serious music-lover would go near it. A key element is the human *interpretation* of the musical symbols. Thus, although the musician is constrained in that he must follow the score, he adds 'feeling' and 'style' to the piece. So here the intention of the composer is not paramount as it was when we considered verbal language. In a sense it doesn't matter, does it, what Beethoven would have heard in his head as he was composing his 9th symphony? It is more compelling to listen to what different conductors and orchestras do with it. All that said, how is it possible for people to judge 'objectively' the performance of musicians in, say, music exams and contests, given that the musical notation is reproduced accurately? Perhaps any explanation of this is beyond words?

We can also speak of the language of art, or at least some sorts of art. In older paintings it was common to include symbols to help convey the artist's 'meaning'. Examples would be a dog to indicate loyalty, a sword to indicate power, an open book to indicate honesty and knowledge. In such works the artist was at pains to *represent* some view of their subject. Certain 'rules' for converting a 3-dimensional subject realistically onto a 2-dimensional canvas were developed along with composition and perspective. It is attention to this method of communicating a meaning to the viewer that engages the brain and conveys knowledge. But we are not all agreed as to how such 'rules' and their application can help justify our judging between different paintings. And in expressionist art, for example, there is no attempt at representing something realistically. We are presented with a composition of lines and shapes to which we respond intellectually and emotionally but not in the medium of words. As with music, perhaps we are not yet advanced enough to be able to interpret such a language as easily as, say, some hieroglyphics. If so, it is a problem of knowledge we leave to future generations of IB students.

**Different verbal languages**
Sign language uses the body, especially the hands, to communicate among the deaf and the non-deaf who have learnt it. Though it might seem odd, this is a verbal language too - and an equally rich one. It is just that, instead of a movement of air particles (sound), we have a movement of the body (sign). That the two are merely different expressions of the same thing is shown by those deaf people who have suffered brain damage: they have difficulties in signing analogous the difficulties with spoken language that the non-deaf-and-brain-damaged have. Perhaps the only limitations would be in their signs for different sounds - and might these be compensated for by their appreciation of the varying styles of signing?

Can one person's language be exactly translated into another's? Optimistically, we might answer '*Yes*'. Consider what we said language is about - the transmission of thoughts via sentences. When we compose a sentence the words contribute to the meaning of the sentence but become transparent to reveal the thought behind it. Surely, all we have to do is translate each word exactly, following the appropriate rules of grammar and, bingo, the thought in the original language will be revealed in another! Unfortunately, if you are trying to translate faithfully, it is not quite as easy as all that. (Fortunately, on the other hand, it is not quite as easy as all that - if you like literature. See next section.)

For one thing there may not be a word in the one language that is a perfect match for the word in the original (what we call in English the *mot juste*). Lots of words have many meanings which depend on the context in which they are used and the type of communication going on. The ancient Greeks, for example, had two verbs for love. One type expressed disinterested love (compassion), the second type expressed the other sorts. Thus the translation of the Greek '*God loves us*' might be more accurately rendered as '*God has compassionate love for us*' but this is rather inadequate and so we settle for the former even though it is inexact.

For another thing, the rules of grammar may not be the same in both languages. I have seen a menu in Portugal with translations into English which offered 'lamb roasted in spit' which, I hope, meant 'spit-roasted lamb'. The difficulties of wrestling one language into the form of another often has the effect of changing what was an elegant sentence in the first into an ordinary, even clumsy, one in a second. Although the meaning is preserved, this would probably do an injustice to the intention of the author of the sentence.

And for another thing, languages contain idioms that, if translated literally, become laughable if not confusing. One might imagine an unhealthy, middle-aged man with a heart condition angrily lashing out with his foot at a metal pail that he has tripped over. This exertion leads directly to a heart-attack which kills him. We could neatly sum this up with the sentence "*He kicked the bucket and kicked the bucket.*" Could one get an exact rendition of this sentence in any other language and still preserve its meaning (including the black humour)?

These difficulties probably mean that something is always lost in translation - the nuances, the echoes, the spirit, whatever you like to call it. On the other hand, something may get added, but it is something that the original did not intend. So far as knowledge is concerned, how can we identify this 'something'? Is it possible for someone who is bilingual to explain the difference? Or is the difference of such a character that it cannot be expressed in the words of one or other language?

This last point - that certain thoughts might *only* be capable of being expressed *in one's own language* - may be crucial (especially when you consider that 96% of the world's languages are spoken by just 4% of the population). If that language died out, then a distinctive way of thinking about the world would be lost. This assumes that the way we think is conditioned, to some extent, by our language. A second assumption is that different languages condition our thinking in different ways. Hence different languages bestow different 'world-views'. Evidence in favour of these assumptions seems clear-cut: when we reflect on things we have an 'inner voice' which uses language to consider, evaluate and so on. This language is our 'native' language, loaded with cultural content; the fact that certain languages lack ways of expressing thoughts that other languages possess indicates that such thoughts never occur (indeed, are incapable of occurring) to some speakers.

Against this we could argue that the 'inner voice' is just a final, conscious, manifestation of thought-processes occurring at a deeper level which is free of words of any language (what we could call a 'mental language') - after all, you can think much faster than you can speak or read. And though it is true that languages vary in their means of expression, that doesn't stop people being intelligible to each other: the thoughts can be appreciated *despite* the incompatible words and the grammar; otherwise, how could we understand the way that people with different languages are different from us?

It is controversial whether a universal language is desirable. On the one side are ranged arguments that language is at the root of culture and helps provide national identity, unity and distinctiveness as well as creating a great breadth of 'world-views' which enriches humanity.

Thus, the knowledge in the world would be diminished with fewer languages. On the other side it is argued that separate languages are divisive in that they exclude non-native speakers and obstruct global intercourse of ideas. And if we chose a language wide and deep enough in vocabulary (and flexible enough in its grammar?) we could develop a richer and more truly international culture; and then knowledge would be advanced more surely and rapidly which would benefit all of humanity.

**Literature**
Literature is not just anything that is written down (except in science where anything that is published is referred to as 'the literature'). Properly, literature is the use of language as a tool that successfully explores and reveals the human condition. It achieves the paradoxical: it uses words alone to convey the knowledge which words alone cannot convey. (An analogy is the television advert showing a television set which has a better-quality picture than the television set you are watching.) How can we get words to do this sort of thing? How can we recognise (and hence *know*) when words are literature and not just the sort of stuff you are reading now?

I suppose if I could answer the first question I'd be polishing my Nobel Literature medal rather than writing this. And answers to the second question will be explored when you discuss the literature you cover in the relevant parts of your IB course. That said, an inkling of what characteristics literature might contain can be briefly illustrated by considering a little bit of Shakespeare. In the play, Hamlet is told by the ghost 'I could tell you a classic horror story'. Well, not in precisely these words. In fact, what the ghost says is:

*I could a tale unfold whose lightest word*
*Would harrow up thy soul, freeze thy young blood,*
*Make thy two eyes like stars start from their spheres,*
*Thy knotted and combined locks to part*
*And each particular hair to stand on end*

*Like quills upon the fretful porpentine.*

Which, I think, is rather better. Shakespeare has not just used more words to get the ghost's intended message across, he uses words and phrases which provoke mental imagery. This is because words have the ambiguity and elasticity which make a complete translation impossible. Just take the word *fretful*. When a porcupine (the word has changed in common usage) is frightened (full of fret or worry), or tormented by an aggressor (worried in a less common use as an active verb), it erects its quills. But doesn't the uncommon word *fretful* sound very like the commoner *frightful* (which might well be one's response to a porcupine 'at bay' - especially if you believe that the animal could fire its quills at you)? Thus the similarity sets up an echo. One could go further still - frightful is another word for *horrid*. And horrid means not just frightful but, literally, *covered with spines...* Did Shakespeare *mean* all of these? Perhaps. Or he may have had the genius to use words and constructions which had such *possibilities* as these.

In any event, I merely point out that certain dimensions of our knowledge of humankind seem to be capable of expression only in the poems, prose and plays in literature or, perhaps, in other aesthetic channels.

# ETHICS

*Fine feathers make fine birds.*

Ethics looks at human behaviour in terms of good and bad, right and wrong. How do we gain knowledge about these sorts of things? Further questions might be: *'What is the point in gaining moral knowledge?'* or *'What's in it for me?'* or even *'What's in it for us?'* Before launching ourselves into some of the responses to such questions, we must make an assumption: we have free will.

**Free will**
This means that we can make real choices about what we do. To be able to make a real choice between two morally different courses of action we must be capable of thinking good thoughts *and* bad thoughts and imagining what their outcomes would be. If you only ever had *good* thoughts you couldn't possibly choose to do bad things, could you? You would be like a robot running on a 'saintly' programme. Thus, even the saintliest people must have 'bad thoughts'. Their saintliness consists in constantly rejecting them and acting on (or reflecting on?) the 'good' ones.

Moral knowledge lies in recognising what I've been calling 'good and bad thoughts' and identifying how they arise as well as what we should then do about them. Recognition comes through what is called our moral sense, an attribute that is seen as exclusively human. Indeed, those figures from the pages of crime or history whom we judge as lacking any moral sense are often described as *inhuman*.

**Moral sense**
It can be argued that there are two distinct parts to this. The first consists of the thoughts and desires that we have in our heads. Thus, I might have the belief that giving money to a charity is a good thing to

do. The second is the action itself: in this case, handing the money over. Evidence that these are distinct comes from the fact that belief in the first does not mean I will automatically carry out the second. Many people would argue that it is the second part, the *action*, which is all-important. They would say that anybody can be a saint in their own mind in just the same way that anybody can fly, move mountains or be hugely popular in their own mind. (And, of course, we can behave monstrously in our own minds too, if we like; and this is unimportant.) To such people our moral sense consists of what we *do* rather than what we think we'd do. Thus, dear reader, we are always honest, fine, open, kind, gentle, genial and generous because we know such things are right; and we don't kill, steal, lie, cheat, bully, boast or bitch because we know such things are wrong.

Where does our moral sense come from? Some have tried to explore this by investigating our language. The basic rationale behind this is that language underpins *all* our thought proceses including those involved in our moral sense. To such people the most inportant questions centre on what we *mean* when we say something is 'good'. This has not proved a fruitful approach largely because words are not enough to describe what we really mean when we say '*It is good to give to charity*'. The words we use always seem to have an emotional content, something to do with our feelings and not just our language.

Such a consideration has led others to claim that our moral sense stems solely from our emotions (and is a type of intuitive thinking as described in the Intuition section in part I). We have certain desires (or emotions, or passions) with respect to other things in the world and these desires motivate us. There are two sorts of motivating desires. The first, stronger, sort are to do with self-interest where we seek outcomes that will benefit us; the second, fainter, sort are based on sympathetic feelings for other people where we consider outcomes that will benefit them. It is claimed that this sympathy for others is natural to human beings. Further, it is claimed to be a natural disposition to discount one's own feelings and reflect impartially on the world. On reflecting in this way, we see that the sympathy we have for others is reinforced by the agreement of other people and this 'summing' of our faint sympathies for others provides a strong public moral code.

The problem with this account is that it diminishes the role of reason to a position that is subservient to the emotions. Further, do we really have an inborn sympathy for others? If we do, then do we all have the same amount (if so, why aren't we all equally good?). If we don't have the same amount, then can we be held responsible if we only have a tiny bit and so behave badly most of the time?

Objections like these have led others to reject this idea of emotion as lying at the heart of our moral sense. Instead, they see it as deriving from our powers of reasoning. The first thing they point out is that there is nothing that separates the thought and the action: it makes no sense to give to charity and yet believe that it is not right to give to charity, for instance. Our actions are thus obeying inner commands (or imperatives). However, we can reason about outcomes of our actions and this reasoning is objectively valid since it will apply to *all* rational beings regardless of their individual desires. Since we arrive at this validity without considering the individual circumstances of other rational beings we can know that our inner commands are valid in just the same way that we know that the laws of reasoning and logic are valid. Reason goes on to tell you to act after discounting 'individual circumstances' because it is more certain that the truth (what would be the *really* right action) applies to everyone, irrespective of their circumstances. Thus, your action is referred to your reasoning and your conclusions will provide a moral code. Your reason also commands you to respect reasoning in others and hence you are led on to a community where reason dictates that every right is respected and every duty is fulfilled.

The criticism of reason being central to our moral sense is that it is hard to see how reason gives you the original motive to act in a good (or bad) way. It also can't explain our feelings about dilemmas. If I unfairly punish a student in the certain knowledge that it will improve life generally this does not stop me feeling bad about being unfair. This is unlike reasoning where a false (or inadequate) solution is easily, carelessly, discounted.

Finally, our moral sense could be the result of training. Granted, we have natural desires that provide us with motives for behaving in a certain way. But these desires can be educated over time. If you resist them, they will grow weaker; if you indulge them, they will grow stronger. This shifts the question of behaviour away from 'What shall I do now?' to 'What sort of moral character should I acquire?' and so stresses the importance of the role of other people and individual circumstance in determining how we behave. It also shifts the emphasis away from '*absolutely* the right thing to do' and towards 'the right thing to do in this situation'. But can there be more than one set of moral truths?

## Moral truth

You might come across the argument that our moral truths are, in fact, just moral values that are only 'true' for our culture or society. If we accept this view, then we have no right to condemn another culture or society for contravening them. Thus, being outraged about slave-owners in the Ancient Greece, witch-burners in Old Europe, ritual torturers of adolescents in Modern Africa, is inappropriate. Such a view might afford us some comfort in that it disallows current and future criticisms from outside our own society. The problem with such an argument is that it is illogical. Rehearsing the lines of argument from the Reason section we might frame it like this:

**Andrew:** *"When it comes to moral truths, every society is right."*
**Barbara:** *"On the contrary, only my society's moral truths are right."*

Clearly, these two statements are contradictory and so they cannot both be right. If Andrew is right, then Barbara must be right too since

Barbara is one of 'every society'. Thus Andrew cannot be right. (Barbara *could* be right but it could also be that both Andrew *and* Barbara are wrong.)

There is a claim that there are certain things in the moral world that are absolutely right or absolutely wrong. By this we mean that irrespective of time, place, culture and circumstance there are some things that are right and some that are wrong and that these apply to all human beings. Two examples that seem to meet this claim might be: 'It is always right to help the needy' and 'It is always wrong to be cruel to people for pleasure'. If we allow this claim for absolute moral truths, then we can feel justified in criticising other cultures and societies. We might also feel that there are more moral truths out there to discover if we have the will and ingenuity to do so. This would give us a target to aim for.

**The aim of moral knowledge**
It is understood that having moral knowledge will help people to behave in a better way. You might have asked yourself *'What is the point in behaving well?'* The most satisfying answer to this is *'Because it is right.'* When you do the right thing you experience a positive sensation in your mind. When you do the wrong thing you experience a negative sensation. These positive sensations have been identified in different ways: a sense of honour; pleasure; fulfilment of the will; fitness with reason. As have the negative ones: shame; pain; self-abasement; contradiction of reason. You will notice that these provide different rationales for behaving in a particular way.

The one aim of behaving well that has derived most support is the aim of happiness. This is something that it makes no sense to question. *'Why do you want to be happy?'* would strike most of us as a silly question - *of course* we want to be happy. Happiness is thus an end in itself. Our reason, or our natural sympathy, or our regard for others in our society, ensures that we try to extend this to as many people as we can.

There have been dissenting voices to happiness as the proper aim of humanity and these choose to emphasise the will of the individual as paramount. They argue that life in all its richness and glory is only truly achieved through the exercise and fulfilment of the will and the striving for excellence through conflict. This is not without interest, but requires a more careful treatment than I have space for here.

**Good behaviour**
If we can't be *sure* about any of the above approaches being the whole truth, how are we to decide what we should do? Well, there are strategies available to help you. You could do as you are told; do what you please; do what is virtuous; do what most other people would do; do what you think best; do what someone else thinks best. But what could guide you as to *which* of these you should choose though?

Let's take a case and look at it from a few different perspectives. Assume a teacher asks you whether they should kick a student or not. What sorts of arguments might you use to convince her that student-kicking is wrong?

**Authority**
There are certain forms of authority to which we might appeal.
*a) "It's against the rules."*
In favour of this approach we might say that rules are made up by our superiors (in terms of age, strength, fire-power, money, etc.) and they know what is best. I trust you find this argument unconvincing. I'm sure you can think of rules that are themselves wrong (like a rule saying you are not permitted to criticise those in authority, for instance). Rules are usually there just to make some institution or other run effectively - they are a convenience. In the past, many people have endured punishment or have died in the belief that there are bad rules (or laws) which ought not to be obeyed. When we say that a rule is good or bad we are appealing to something outside the rule itself: whether it is *indeed* right or wrong.

*b) "My Holy Book says it is wrong."*
In favour of this is that a supernatural source of the truth cannot be wrong. However, notwithstanding that following a prescription for life unquestioningly seems to contradict the idea of free will, this cuts no ice with someone who does not share your particular faith. We would still like to say the student-kicker is wrong even if we had no faith at all.

**Personal knowledge**
*"I know it is wrong."*
In favour of this approach is our ability to consult our own minds or, if we are appealing to intuitive knowledge, we are more likely to say 'our own hearts'. We just *know* that it is a bad thing to kick another person. Unfortunately, the student-kicker could say that in her heart *she* knows that kicking students is good, and there the argument would have to rest.

**Personal reaction**
*"It does not please me when I think of it and so it is wrong."*
This tunes into our intuitive knowledge and expresses our view as a human being. We assume that other members of our species share this view. But the student-kicker could again retort that it pleases *them*. Or they could say that pleasure, or happiness, is not a sufficient explanation for dictating behaviour.

**Knowledge from the majority**
*"Most people agree with me that it's wrong."*
This is based on the idea that when a lot of people believe something then that makes it more likely to be true. But does the above statement count as knowledge, or is it mere opinion? And history has shown that truth does not always follow the majority. For example, in the past the majority of people thought that the keeping of slaves was morally acceptable (including many of the slaves themselves).

## Appealing to self-interest
*"How would you like it if you were a student and someone did that to you?"*
This seems a brilliant question. Of course it assumes that the student-kicker is human and appreciates that other rational beings exist. It asks them to discount their personal desires and consider other people sympathetically. One hopes that humans are capable of this. If not sympathy, then reason will show them that being kicked is painful, humiliating and inappropriate. Hence it should not be visited on anyone, hence it is wrong. They might resist this line of argument, however, saying that the aim of their life is excellence. And, for them, this consists of the exercise of their will, which includes characteristics like courage, pride and firmness, and the suppression of any weaknesses like pity and charity. Thus this sort of person would reject our notion that all rational beings should be treated equally. Also, can we (or should we?) treat everyone in the world in the same way? Is it *possible* for you to treat a stranger in exactly the same way that you would treat a friend or a loved one? If not, then why pretend it is?

## Consider the consequences
*"Kicking students makes the world a worse place"*
We might ignore our desires (or intentions) when it comes to moral questions and look only towards the consequences of our actions. This side-steps the slippery problems above and gives us a reason for behaving in a particular way (provided, of course, we agree on the sort of consequences that are desirable). We might argue that physical chastisement will lead to the victim losing self-esteem, becoming brutalised and thus more likely to be physically violent; and promote a climate of fear which is not conducive to good relationships, and so on. They might argue that these are sloppy arguments based on sloppy thinking - where is any conclusive evidence to support the claims? And how are you going to measure the degree of 'worseness' in the world? Do we measure it now? in ten minutes? next year? These questions seem very hard (if not impossible) to answer satisfactorily.

Emphasising the importance of the *consequences* of our actions leads to what might be regarded as unfairness. To show this, we need to employ a thought-experiment. This is because you have to imagine a man in two identical circumstances at the same moment with just one difference. This is impossible to obtain in the real world but simple for the brain. Imagine a man parks his car on a slight slope and gets out forgetting to set the hand-brake. He locks the doors and walks away. A few minutes later a lorry goes past and puts the man's car in motion and it runs down the slope. I want you to imagine that happening twice identically. The only difference is the outcome. In the first case the car runs down the slope, over a pavement and into a wall doing damage only to the man's car. In the second case the car runs into a young child walking on the pavement in front of the wall and kills her. What should happen to the man?

If you look at the consequences (which is the over-riding element in British law, at least) then, in the first case, the man would probably get a small fine for negligence. In the second case, he will be tried for manslaughter and may well be sent to prison. But if you look at it from the point of view of the man's *intention* (for which he can be held to be responsible) then he has obviously done the same thing wrong in both cases: not set the hand-brake. He *ought* to have remembered but he did not. And if he has done the same thing wrong then he should get the same punishment no matter what the consequences (either the fine or the prison sentence). He had no control over what was in the path of his car, he was just lucky that it hit the wall, or unlucky that it hit the girl. And surely it is unfair to punish someone on the basis of whether they are lucky or not?

### Doing what's reasonable
*"Kicking students is unreasonable"*
We can make a final appeal to reason here (as outlined in the section about moral sense). We can argue that reason is the final arbiter and over-rides any other sort of justification. Even if some-one argues

that it is a cultural tradition in their society that students are kicked by teachers, we can still ask them for a reason; and their reply will have to be in terms of reason rather than their culture.

This very brief treatment gives you a clue as to the problems associated with 'doing the right thing'. The two main approaches to ethical questions are through considering either the intention of the individual, or the consequences of the action: *"Should I do this because it is right in itself regardless of the consequences?"* or *"Should I do this because the consequences of doing it are better than those of not doing it?"* Of course, it may be that these two strands of thinking are analogous to a piece of rope: two rope strands twisted together make a rope that can carry a greater weight than the two strands used separately.

Exploring different moral questions with these perspectives in mind with fellow-students and (I hope, nonkicking) teachers will help you clarify your own individual reaction to moral questions. This is especially important as our ethical considerations give force to the idea of human (and perhaps animal?) rights and may help to elucidate problems where such individual rights are in conflict either with each other, or between individuals, or between groups, or with the interests of the state.

# AESTHETICS

*Eagles don't catch flies.*


Along with our moral sense and language, our appreciation of the arts sets us apart from all other species. Architecture, paintings, sculpture and music are often used to indicate the degree of our civilization as individuals and as societies. As such, they are of huge importance: a lack of appreciation of the arts marks out a person or a group as culturally impoverished, as having not fully realised their potential for being human.

I have used the word *appreciation* advisedly. It is not enough to have mere *knowledge* of the arts - who did the composing/painting and when, and so on, (though this is necessary when discussing the arts, if not when creating art itself). You have to have an *understanding* of a work of art in a way that is said to be quite different from an understanding of, say, a mathematical formula or the grammar of a sentence. Because this understanding is so different, we turn to a concept that is rather like the 'sixth sense' we refer to when we become aware of something that we feel has entered our thoughts by a route other than via one or more of the usual five senses. That concept is the *aesthetic sense*. It is something we will have to consider before going on to look at what we can make of knowledge in the arts.

**The aesthetic sense**
Our sense of vision responds to light. Our sense of touch responds to the feel of an object. What does our aesthetic sense respond to? The classical answer is 'beauty' and we'll explore this first.

It is hard to imagine a human being who could not be moved by some sort of *natural* beauty - someone who could gaze on a sunset and see just clouds, sky and colours; someone who could listen to a skylark's song but hear just the notes and phrasing. We would think such a person was not normal because being moved by such things appears to be a fundamental human attribute. If you cannot experience a sense of beauty then your humanity itself is called into question. (This really points up the difference between the 'aesthetic sense' and the five physical senses because one can lose one or more of these senses and still be counted as fully human - blind people, for example, can appreciate birdsong, deaf people sunsets.)

So, let's assume that humans do have such an appreciation of the beauty in Nature. Where does it come from? The most straight-forward answer is to say that it must be inborn, that there must be some part of the brain that gives us a sort of pleasure when stimulated by various types of natural beauty. It is possible to argue that this could constitute a human characteristic that would be of survival value - a particular landscape could 'inform' us that this is a good place to camp; a particular birdsong could 'inform' us of good hunting nearby. But these seem rather feeble explanations of something that is such a forceful and dominant feature of our brains. What possible 'survival value' could there be derived from gazing enraptured at the changing colours in a sunset?

It could still be inborn but *accidental* in the same way (as already mentioned in the section on Intuition). Certain mental impressions get routed to the part of the brain that registers a feeling of pleasure for no particular reason at all - it's just the way the brain has grown up. Again, this seems unsatisfactory because our sense of the aesthetic is so powerfully human that ascribing it to accident would trivialise it - our culture can be regarded as *depending* on our aesthetic sense so how can it be just a chance feature?

A third possibility is that we *learn* our appreciation of natural beauty from other people. This seems hard to concede. Although your parents might say "*Isn't that a beautiful sunset?*" you would need to have a sense of what is beautiful in the first place to appreciate what they meant by 'beautiful'. This is like someone explaining a joke to you that you have failed to find amusing - you can *understand* where the funniness lies but still not laugh. Your parents could *tell* you why something was beautiful until they were blue in the face but what they cannot do is make you *appreciate* the beauty itself. This implies that you cannot be *reasoned* into an appreciation of beauty; it must appeal to you intuitively or emotionally. I'll return to this point more fully later.

A fourth possibility is that a part of our minds is wholly free from rational thinking - a part which stems our imagination, our creativity, our noble passions. It is *this* part of our mind to which the aesthetic appeals and, given its immunity to rational thought, we should abandon all pretence at trying to 'understand' it in rational terms. But why should any part of our nature be immune to reason? Surely we all want to have reasons as to why one thing is beautiful and another is not? If we abandon reason here, then beauty becomes anything that anyone wants to call it.

Since none of the above seem to be at all satisfactory, we might say that the fifth possibility is that there is a fifth possibility - one we are (at present) unable to formulate. Perhaps the appreciation of natural beauty is, like morality and language, such a complex mix of senses, minds and society that we are only just beginning to disentangle some of its attributes.

All that said, if we take it for granted that there is such a thing as an aesthetic sense that appreciates natural beauty, is this the same sense that is appealed to when we are exposed to a piece of *artificial* beauty, like a painting by Turner or a piece by Vaughan Williams? In the interests of economy at least, we might say yes - why would there be different parts of the brain for appreciating what seem to be identical sorts of sensations? However, although we might all agree that appreciating a sunset is something that all humans can do, appreciating a *painting* of a sunset does not fall into the same category at all. People disagree (often quite violently) about whether one work of art is more lor less appealing than another. This disagreement has led to a questioning of the idea of art as being a capturing, exploration and presentation of the beautiful. Has beauty got anything at all to do with art?

**Art and beauty**
The answer to the question is: It depends on what you mean. Some would argue that what is beautiful depends entirely on the individual. In favour of this view we could claim that our aesthetic sense is intensely emotional and personal; what appeals to us as being beautiful is incapable of being analysed and categorised. In addition, an aesthetic sense cannot be experienced at second hand; you must perceive it *yourself* to appreciate it aesthetically. Thus it must be wholly subjective. Moreover, the art which has appealed to different societies in different times has had nothing in common. There is nothing that is fundamental to art except its appeal to an individual's aesthetic sense. We merely choose to call this appeal 'beauty' because it's a handy term. Following this line of argument we could define art as 'anything that appeals to the aesthetic sense'. (And the aesthetic sense as 'that which is stimulated by art'.) Though circular, at least this has the virtue of honesty: we acknowledge that a simple definition of art is not possible. Having done so we are then free to explore this fundamental human sense by challenging it with a variety of artistic possibilities. Art can be a way of exploring the nonrational, the intuitive, part of the mind. If we accept this view of art, then we have to acknowledge that *anything* can qualify as a work of art just so long as it appeals to *someone's* aesthetic sense.

On the other hand, we could say that to qualify as art something should have certain attributes and thus 'appealing to the aesthetic sense' is too loose and subjective to be of any use at all. If we allowed this as a definition, then if you looked at a painting by Vermeer and it left you cold, but then you looked at a painting by me and you thought 'Wow!', you would have to say that, for you, I was a better artist than

Vermeer (which, I assure you, is not true). The mistake here, it is said, is concentrating exclusively on the aesthetic sense. What you have to do is ignore this and *concentrate on the object itself* and try to discern what is appealing about it. If this angle is pursued, then many people would claim that it *is* possible to judge art objectively, that there *are* criteria for deciding on the relative merits of works of art and hence of artists. This implies that there are standards in art of which we can have knowledge. Evidence in favour of this view is that the aesthetic sense can be *developed*. That is, you can learn more about those attributes that constitute good art rather than bad art (or no art at all). And if you can learn about such things then this strongly implies that such things exist. This is why people go to art or music school, for instance; not just to learn technique and the facts about artists, but to develop their sense of the aesthetic. Thus artists in the broadest sense (including architects, musicians and even critics) know more about what constitutes good art than those of us who have neglected this side of our education.

In reply (or in defence) we might reply by saying that such artists have been indoctrinated into believing in certain 'aesthetic values' which are as empty of meaning as the word 'beauty'. *"I know a good piece of art when I see or hear it and I don't need any explanation for it because any explanation is going to be an unnecessary and threadbare load of old flannel."*

I leave the controversy unresolved. Some artists explore the rational side of aesthetics - searching for the fundamental attributes of art such as proportion, form and harmony, for example. Some explore the irrational side - the mind's attributes that appear untamed, unbidden and inexplicable. Others combine them. What does seem clear is that we cannot be sure how many aspects art has. They seem to range from nought to infinity.

**Knowledge and aesthetics**
It might seem from all I've said that there is little 'knowledge' to be

had in aesthetics; that, although we might like to claim that one building is sublime and another is hideous, we cannot appeal to anything objective to justify our claim. We certainly cannot appeal to what the majority of people think as a justification. It seems that most people have little aesthetic sense and those that do will generally retreat from argument since they know that an aesthetic argument is unwinnable. And anyway, history has shown us that the majority has been 'wrong' in the past - few people appreciated the art of Van Gogh in his lifetime but he is very popular nowadays.

Compared with many other subjects, philosophers have added little to our knowledge of aesthetics. This is a pity since aesthetics is one of the activities that gives a sense to human life. It has been argued that when contemplating an object aesthetically we are going beyond selfish interests and regarding something *for its own sake*. When we do this sort of thing we enter an *aesthetic* world, one imbued with importance and meaning all its own that cannot be directly referred to the 'real' world. Contrast this world with the one where unalloyed self-interest rules - going to work to earn money, earning money to buy a car, buying a car to impress one's friends... When you reflect on the latter doesn't it seem as senseless as the cow going to the field to eat grass, eating grass to grow larger, growing larger to be able to reproduce, reproducing to have little cows... that go to fields to eat grass...?

The world where we contemplate objects for their own sake has been identified with that key human attribute, reason. Perhaps, if we all put in more time and effort in developing our powers of reasoning, our lives would not only be fuller and richer but we might also be able to talk more knowledgeably about aesthetic values. If nothing else, we could regard the world more wisely.

# Acknowledgments

Firstly, I must thank the Headmaster and Governors of Sevenoaks School for providing me with the time and encouragement to write this book.

Many colleagues at the school have helped to elucidate and clarify the ideas I have set out. I should particularly like to record my thanks to the following for offering criticisms and improvements to the various sections when in early drafts: Sue Austin, Ollie Barratt, Maureen Connelly, Andrew Forbes, John Guyatt, Gregory Klyve, Janet Thomas, Brenda Walpole.

I owe a great debt of gratitude to my father-in-law, Duncan Stuart, for correcting my English and my grammar - and almost curing me of the inappropriate dash.

Finally, my wife, Arabella, supported my efforts throughout the period of producing this book and listened to my endless explanations and justifications with great forbearance and great good humour.